MY IDENTITY IN CHRIST

STUDENT EDITION

C. GENE WILKES

LifeWay Press®
Nashville, Tennessee

ISBN: 978-0-6330-2992-0
Item 001051020

This book is a resource in the Personal Life
category of the Christian Growth Study Plan.
Course: CG-0582

Dewey Decimal Classification Number: 248.83
Subject Heading: CHRISTIAN LIFE

Printed in the United States of America

Student Ministry Publishing
LifeWay Church Resources
One LifeWay Plaza
Nashville, TN 37234-0174

We believe that the Bible has God for its author; salvation for its end; and truth,
without any mixture of error, for its matter and that all Scripture is totally true and trustworthy.
The 2000 statement of *The Baptist Faith and Message* is our doctrinal guideline.

CONTENTS

MEET C. GENE WILKES

C. Gene Wilkes is married to Kim (McHan) Wilkes and is the father of two daughters, Storey and Summer. He is the pastor of Legacy Church, Plano, Texas, where he has served since 1987. The church has made several significant changes during Gene's ministry in order to more effectively carry out its mission to make disciples. Materials like *My Identity in Christ, Student Edition* are used at Legacy to help members become disciples who "Worship, Reach, Connect, Grow, and Serve." The church's vision is to become a mission outpost where every member is a missionary in his or her mission field.

Gene is the author of *Jesus on Leadership, Student Edition* a LifeWay interactive workbook and a Tyndale trade book by the same name. Gene has also written *With All My Soul: God's Design for Spiritual Wellness* and *Paul on Leadership.* He is a national and international conference speaker on the topics of servant leadership, spiritual gifts, and transitioning churches to become more mission-field focused.

Gene received his bachelor's degree from Baylor University and his M.Div. and Ph.D. from Southwestern Baptist Theological Seminary in Fort Worth, Texas. His hobbies are reading, writing, running, and golf.

INTRODUCTION

My Identity in Christ, Student Edition is about your identity, who you are before God and others. It is about how who you are in Christ affects every part of your life—from how you think and feel to the choices you make each day. *My Identity in Christ, Student Edition* will help you discover how you can have a vital relationship with Jesus Christ and actually become like Him in every aspect of your life. Why is this so important?

1. This study is important to you as a teen because you are in the process of becoming an adult. In these years of adolescence you will discover how God has made you. You will gain confidence in your skills and talents. You will form your own opinions and ideas about life. You will discover work and hobbies you will enjoy the rest of your life. In the middle of this process, you will develop a concept of who you are as a person. This is your identity.

A predominant way of thinking about identity in our culture is to focus on how you esteem, or, value yourself. We call this self-esteem, and it is your perception of your worth and value as an individual. According to some, how you value yourself determines whether you succeed or fail in life. The source of self-esteem is your own personal thinking about who you are. Much has been made of the importance of convincing yourself how valuable and worthy you are.

The trap of self-esteem is that you make this judgment of yourself by yourself. Some say a personal goal should be to overcome all external ideas of who you are by choosing how you would like to see yourself. Any source or authority is open for acceptance. This unchecked search for self-worth can lead to closely-held but incorrect ideas about yourself. An extreme example of this way of thinking has led some people to believe that they are either god-like or that they are actually gods themselves. Christians must avoid falling into the trap of determining their self-worth based only on what they think or feel from their personal perspective. Christians find their worth and purpose in life from trusting the love of God shown in Christ Jesus and the power of the Holy Spirit's presence in their lives.

2. The second reason this study is important for you is that many followers of Jesus do not understand the goal of their Christian life— to be like Jesus. The Bible states, *"We, who with unveiled faces all reflect the Lord's glory, are being transformed into his likeness with ever-increasing glory, which comes from the Lord, who is the Spirit"* (2 Cor. 3:18).

This workbook will guide you through the teachings of Jesus and other passages in the Bible to help you know Christ and how that affects all you do and think. You will spend time each day for the next six weeks prayerfully studying and putting into your daily life the biblical teachings about who Jesus is and who you are in Him. You will meet each week with a small group of people we will call your "Identity Group." Here you will share what you learned in your study of God's Word between each meeting. You will learn to love and support these Christian brothers and sisters as each of you are "being transformed into His likeness."

WEEK 1
WHO IS THIS JESUS?

This week you will ...
- take time to answer the question, "Who am I?" (Day 1);
- answer the most important question Jesus will ask you, "Who do you say I am?" (Day 2);
- discover who Jesus is by examining what He said about Himself (Day 3);
- examine several of the names of Jesus and how they describe His identity (Day 4); and,
- discover how knowing who Jesus is will allow you to become like Him (Day 5).

Memory Verse
"On that day you will realize that I am in my Father, and you are in me, and I am in you. Whoever has my commands and obeys them, he is the one who loves me. He who loves me will be loved by my Father, and I too will love him and show myself to him" (John 14:20-21).

"Since I became a Christian, I don't know how to act," she said. "I realize now that the people I used to run around with are really mean to each other. I don't feel a part of them anymore. It's like I am a different person. I don't know whether to correct them and make them mad at me, or just pull out and leave them alone—but, I don't think that is what God wants me to do. Those people are my life. What can I do to help them know what I know?"

This teen's question was a result of her trust in Christ and her desire to live like Jesus. As Christ's teachings and presence filled her life, she could see how her old ways of living were wrong. God put a desire in her heart to help her friends, even though they sometimes rejected her. This student was experiencing spiritual transformation, and it was affecting everything she had known before that event.

The Bible says we are being transformed into the Lord's likeness. Spiritual transformation is God's work of changing a believer into the likeness of Jesus by creating a new identity in Christ and by empowering a lifelong relationship of love, trust, and obedience to glorify God.

God's desire is for you to become like Jesus. Max Lucado said it this way, "God loves you just the way you are, but he refuses to leave you that way. ... He wants you to be just like Jesus."[1] Being just like Jesus begins with knowing who Jesus is and who you are in relationship with Him, and that's what we will do this week as we answer the question, Who is this Jesus?

[1]*Just Like Jesus*, Max Lucado, 1998, Word Publishing, Nashville, Tennessee. All rights reserved.

DAY 1

WHO AM I?

What is man that you are mindful of him,
the son of man that you care for him?
(Ps. 8:4).

TODAY YOU WILL ...

○ review popular concepts of personal identity;
○ examine four categories of influences that form your identity;
○ read biblical passages about who you are before God; and,
○ examine the biblical concepts of identity.

Begin this study by making a list of names some students use to identify others. Examples may include "freak" or "jock."
List answers below:

_____
_____
_____
_____
_____

You may use some of these names to identify yourself. These titles help answer the question, "Who am I?" According to social scientists and psychologists, your answer to that question is the foundation of who you are. It's your identity. Psychologists tell us that answering the identity question is what maturity is all about. They say that your answer reveals whether or not you trust who you are.

Your answer to that question, however, is not the most important answer in your life. The most important question you will ever answer is Jesus' question to you, "Who do you say I am?" Why is that the most important question? Your answer to Jesus' question about who He is determines your spiritual identity, your true identity. This identity determines everything about your life now and for eternity. In this session, we will consider different ways to answer the question, "Who am I?"

Fingerprints and Godprints

Let's take a moment and see how the world we live in has answered the identity question. Then, we will see how the Bible answers it.

First, your fingerprints are unique to you. This is why law enforcement agencies use them for identification. Fingerprints are created by your genetic code, your DNA (deoxyribonucleic acid). No two codes are alike, unless you're an identical twin. Your DNA determines everything from eye color to the shape of your body. It also influences your athletic and mental abilities. Your *fingerprints* tell who you are physically.

Second, your social environment also has an influence on your identity. I call this influence your *parentprints*. Your parents helped mold your behavior, value system, and sense of worth. They gave you your name, a very important part of who you are. These "prints" have a lasting effect on who you are. Unlike your fingerprints, however, these prints can be altered and new ones added. Some believe that social environment has an irreversible impact on who you are in the world. These people would disregard the biblical concept of being transformed into the likeness of Jesus.

A third aspect of who you are is what I call *lifeprints*. These are the influences that mold who you are by your choices and the events that happen to and around you. These prints are the result of decisions such as whether or not to steal, where to go to college, what job to take, and whether or not to marry. You carve these prints as you make choices. Each decision you make creates a series of events that can affect how you see yourself and how you value what you do. Lifeprints are also the result of events that happen to you. Disease, abuse, and criminal or civil activity all can leave lasting prints on your identity. Many people allow circumstances to determine how they feel about themselves. For instance, a good day may mean things are going your way and you are happy. A bad day may be when circumstances do not go the way you planned or wanted them to go. You may allow daily events to influence how you feel about yourself. This is not biblical thinking.

If this were a secular book, we would stop with these three influences and declare that they make up your identity. But, the world overlooks the most important influence on a person's identity. This is what I call *Godprints,* the influence of God on your life. From birth to eternity, God influences who you are and what you become. God forms you genetically, allows or ordains events to happen, and offers opportunities of grace and salvation to you. As you respond in faith to God, He forms a print of His presence on your life.

Steven Curtis Chapman celebrates the "fingerprints of God" in a song by the same name. The lyrics to the chorus are: "I can see the fingerprints of God/When I look at you/I can see the fingerprints of God/And I know it's true/You're a masterpiece/That all creation quietly applauds/And you're covered with the fingerprints of God."[1]

⊕ **Answer the question, "Who am I?" using the descriptions on the previous page. Write descriptive statements about yourself under each heading in the margin.**

Cars, Houses, and Schools, Oh My!

Another way we answer the question "Who am I?" is by adding up what we have acquired and accomplished and then comparing ourselves to others. The influence of materialism causes many cultures to determine who a person is by external things. We most often believe that more is better and that the accumulation of wealth (things, power, influence) determines the value and worth of an individual. Some people trust the other extreme that "less is more" and judge people by their lack of accumulated wealth.

⊕ **Here are some ways you may compare yourself and what you have with others. Place a check by the phrase that best completes the statement. Be prepared to share your answers in your Identity Group.**

I tend to evaluate who I am based on …
○ **the clothes I wear.**
○ **the car I drive and the house I live in.**
○ **what others say about me.**
○ **my class rank.**
○ **who my friends are.**
○ **what I look like.**
○ **the clubs and organizations I belong to.**
○ **what I believe about myself.**

These things can form the basis of your identity. They can also form the foundation upon which you build your worth and value to others. God, however, has a different way of determining our worth and identity.

It's the Heart

You and I tend to let appearance and wealth determine who we are. God evaluates who we are in a different way.

⊕ **Read 1 Samuel 16:1-7.**

What was Samuel, the prophet, seeking to do? _____
_____
_____
_____
_____

When Samuel saw Jesse's son Eliab, what did he think? *(v. 6)* _____
_____
_____

Fingerprints
_____
_____
_____
_____
_____

Parentprints
_____
_____
_____
_____
_____

Lifeprints
_____
_____
_____
_____
_____

Godprints
_____
_____
_____
_____
_____

When they arrived, Samuel saw Eliab and thought, "Surely the Lord's anointed stands here before the Lord." But the Lord said to Samuel, "Do not consider his appearance or his height, for I have rejected him. The Lord does not look at the things man looks at. Man looks at the outward appearance, but the Lord looks at the heart" (1 Sam. 16:6-7).

What was God's response? *(v. 7)*

_____

_____

_____

_____

After God withdrew His favor from King Saul, God sent Samuel to anoint a new king. God sent him to Bethlehem and to the family of Jesse. God had chosen one of Jesse's sons as the next king. When Samuel saw Jesse's oldest son, Eliab, he was convinced God had chosen him as the next king. He must have been tall and handsome like King Saul. But, God corrected the prophet's thinking. God said to Samuel, *"Do not consider his appearance or his height, for I have rejected him. The Lord does not look at the things man looks at. Man looks at the outward appearance, but the Lord looks at the heart"* (1 Sam. 16:7).

"The Lord looks at the heart." Your heart is where God looks for your identity. While people judge themselves and others by appearances, God looks at the heart. Spiritual identity is based on what God sees there.

God's Look at Your Heart

What does God see when He looks at your heart? Since Jesus and God are the same Person, let's look to what Jesus said about our hearts.

> **Read Matthew 15:19. How does Jesus describe the heart?**

> **Read Matthew 6:21. Where is our true identity? Underline your answer in the Scripture**

Jesus knows best how you and I function and who we really are. When Jesus taught His followers about who we are, He described our hearts. Jesus said that *"out of the heart come evil thoughts, murder, adultery, sexual immortality, theft, false testimony, slander"* (Matt. 15:19). All of these sins of self-centeredness hurt others. God knows your heart, and your heart drives you to do things that are unacceptable to God. It deceives you about who you really are.

The source of your sinful heart is a sinful nature. This is at the core of who you are and why you choose to live the way you do. You and I have corrupted spiritual DNA. Your natural code causes you to make choices that hurt others, and these choices separate you from God. As long as your spiritual DNA is without change, you cannot live as God desires you to live, and you cannot see yourself as God sees you. But, how do you get new spiritual DNA?

A Decision You Must Make

The issue of identity comes down to where you put your trust. Do you trust what a secular society says about who you are? Do you allow biological and social influences alone to guide what you believe about yourself? Do you trust what God says about where to look for your true identity and what Jesus says about the condition of your heart?

"Out of the heart come evil thoughts, murder, adultery, sexual immorality, theft, false testimony, slander" (Matt. 15:19).

"Where your treasure is, there your heart will be also" (Matt. 6:21).

The source of your sinful heart is a sinful nature.

How do you gain a new identity that is true to God? You need a new heart, a new identity. You can receive a new identity by receiving new spiritual DNA. This is what salvation is about. You can have new spiritual DNA—a new spiritual code—that guides you to live as God desires and helps you become like Jesus.

The process of receiving new spiritual DNA begins by answering Jesus' question directed to you. It is the same one He asked His disciples. You will have opportunity to answer that question tomorrow.

SUMMARY

- The answer to the question "Who am I?" is important.
- Your fingerprints, parentprints, lifeprints, and Godprints influence who you are.
- God looks on your heart rather than outward appearances to determine your identity.
- Your natural DNA is corrupt and causes you to live outside God's plan for your life.
- You need new spiritual DNA to be what God created you to be.

PERSONAL REFLECTION

✛ **Prayerfully complete these activities in your Identity Journal.**

1. **Based on my answers in this session, what are my current standards for determining my identity?**
2. **Of the four "prints" I read about today, which one has had the most influence on my life? Fingerprints? Parentprints? Lifeprints? Godprints?**
3. **When I read about the condition of my heart from the words of Jesus, I feel …**
4. **If God were to ask me, "Who are you?" how would I answer?**

---

[1]Steven Curtis Chapman, "The Fingerprints of God," *Speechless*, Sparrow Music, 1999.

DAY 2

WHO DO YOU SAY I AM?

"But what about you?" he asked,
"Who do you say I am?"
Simon Peter answered, "You are the Christ,
the Son of the living God" (Matt. 16:15-16).

TODAY YOU WILL ...

○ review Jesus' discussion with His disciples about His identity;
○ list contemporary answers to Jesus' question about His identity;
○ examine Peter's answer to Jesus' question; and,
○ write your response to Jesus' question about His identity.

Yesterday you answered the question, "Who am I?" That is the question of identity. While you acknowledge the importance of the question, it is not the most important question you will answer in life. The most important one you will ever answer is Jesus' question, "Who do you say that I am?" Let's look at the passage of Scripture where Jesus asks His disciples that question.

When Jesus came to the region of Caesarea Philippi, he asked his disciples, "Who do people say the Son of Man is?" (Matt. 16:13-14).

✠ **Read Matthew 16:13-14. Underline Jesus' question to His disciples. What were some of their answers?**

1._____
_____
_____

2._____
_____
_____

3._____
_____

4._____
_____

Jesus asked His closest followers, "Who do people say the Son of Man is?" He did not ask this question to find out what the majority were thinking so He could become those things. Jesus asked the question to discover what the disciples were hearing about Him. He wanted to know if they understood who He really was. They said some thought He was John the Baptist, Elijah, Jeremiah, or one of the prophets. Everyone seemed to have their own opinion. Who Jesus is, however, is not determined by what people think about Him.

⊕ **How do you believe people today would answer the question, "Who is Jesus?" Be prepared to compare your ideas with others in your Identity Group.**

Some people believe Jesus is a religious figure or great teacher. Some see Jesus as a leader of a great revolution or a social reformer. Others would call Him a healer or miracle worker. Some, I'm afraid, would say Jesus is no longer relevant to what is going on in the world. As with the disciple's answers about Jesus, what others say about His identity is not how you know Christ. You know Christ by accepting in faith who Jesus says He is, not what popular opinion says about Him.

⊕ **After hearing His disciples' response, Jesus asked the most important question of one of His followers: "Who do you say I am?" (Matt. 16:15). What was Peter's answer in verse 16?**

Peter stepped up and said, *"You are the Christ, the Son of the living God."* This was the answer Jesus wanted to hear.

⊕ **Read Matthew 16:17-19. Without trying to understand everything fully, what three things did Jesus say to Peter?**

1. _____
_____

2. _____
_____

3. _____
_____
_____

Jesus told Peter that he did not discover this truth on his own *(v. 17)*. Jesus said, *"God bless you, Simon son of Jonah! You didn't get that answer out of books or from teachers. My Father in heaven, God himself, let you in on this secret of who I really am" (The Message).* God reveals the truth of who Jesus is. We cannot completely understand the deep things of God on our own. God reveals Himself to us. And the perfect revelation of God is Jesus.

> *Who Jesus is ... is not determined by what people think about Him.*

> *"What about you?" he asked. "Who do you say I am?" (Matt. 16:15).*

> *Jesus replied, "Blessed are you, Simon son of Jonah, for this was not revealed to you by man, but by my Father in heaven. And I tell you that you are Peter, and on this rock I will build my church, and the gates of Hades will not overcome it. I will give you the keys of the kingdom of heaven; whatever you bind on earth will be bound in heaven, and whatever you loose on earth will be loosed in heaven" (Matt. 16:17-19).*

13

⊕ **Imagine Jesus standing before you and asking you the question, "Who do you say I am?" Write your answer below.**

_____

_____

_____

_____

_____

_____

Was your answer the same as Peter's? How was it different? Peter's confession is the life-changing response Jesus desires of all His followers. Your answer may be the same as Peter's answer, but becoming like Jesus is not just about getting right answers. You can quote the Bible and not know its Author. This was true even of this close follower of Jesus.

> From that time on Jesus began to explain to his disciples that he must go to Jerusalem and suffer many things at the hands of the elders, chief priests and teachers of the law, and that he must be killed and on the third day be raised to life. Peter took him aside and began to rebuke him. "Never, Lord," he said. "This shall never happen to you!" (Matt. 16:21-22).

⊕ **Read Matthew 16:21-22. What did Jesus teach His disciples about what it meant for Him to be the Messiah? Write a brief summary in your Identity Journal.**

After Peter gave Jesus the correct answer about who He was, Jesus took the opportunity to explain what He would do as the Christ. Jesus told them He must go to Jerusalem, suffer, die, and be raised from the dead on the third day. Jesus was reinforcing Peter's confession. The disciple's response to Jesus' description of coming events, however, showed that Peter did not fully understand why Jesus had come.

⊕ **Peter insisted that Jesus would never suffer in the way He described. How did Jesus respond? Read Matthew 16:23 and write your answer below.**

> Jesus turned and said to Peter, "Get behind me, Satan! You are a stumbling block to me; you do not have in mind the things of God, but the things of men" (Matt. 16:23).

Jesus' response to Peter was severe. He called His closest follower "Satan!" Why? Peter had false ideas about who Jesus was as the Messiah, and the Master never allows the servant to define the mission. Jesus had already overcome Satan's temptations to accept shortcuts to the kingdom. Jesus knew He must suffer, and those who followed Him must follow Him to the cross. Peter missed the point that Jesus' identity determined his mission. Who you are is key to what you do with your life.

This is an extremely important point in our study. The Word of God defines your identity in Christ, not your understanding of who you are. You may know all the right answers but misinterpret them. The goal of becoming like Jesus is changing your perceptions and ideas to conform to God's truth. Like Peter, we must allow the Word of God to address our misconceptions about Jesus. Even though it may seem unreasonable (like the Messiah dying on a cross rather than leading an army), we must submit our thoughts to the truth of God. You must be prepared to adjust how you think and how you live to Jesus' pattern for living.

Jesus then taught us how to become His follower and how to become like Him. Even if you know the answer to the most important question posed by Jesus, "Who do you say I am?" you must forsake your perceptions of Jesus and let Him be Lord of your life.

✠ **Read Matthew 16:24. What does Jesus require of those who confess Him as Christ?**

Jesus said to deny self. To deny self means to set your desires and wishes aside to accomplish the purposes of God in your life. This is a daily exercise that allows the things of God to become priorities over personal wishes. So how does this happen? Jesus said it happens by taking up your cross. This is not religious jargon for going to church! Jesus literally meant that you must kill the natural desires of your sinful nature every day.

Jesus concluded His sentence in *Matthew 16:24* with, follow me. *Give up what you want, kill the ego, and follow me* is the essence of Jesus' teaching about being His disciple. The way you become like Jesus is to follow Him in every aspect of your life. You will receive more information about how to follow Jesus later in this study. For now, test your heart to see if you are willing to move forward to discover the biblical answer to Jesus' question, "Who do you say I am?"

> *Then Jesus said to his disciples, "If anyone would come after me, he must deny himself and take up his cross and follow me (Matt. 16:24).*

SUMMARY

○ Jesus' most important question to you is, "Who do you say I am?"
○ The God-revealed answer is, "You are the Christ, the Son of the living God."
○ God's truth, not your personal ideas, defines Christ's identity and His mission.
○ To become like Jesus, you must deny your selfish desires, put your personal wishes on the cross, and follow Him.
○ You can become like Jesus when you trust who He says He is and what He says He will do.

PERSONAL REFLECTION

✠ **Prayerfully complete the following activities.**

1. **Do I accept in faith who Jesus is?** ○ Yes ○ Not sure
2. **Even though I have confessed Jesus is the Christ, the Son of the living God, I still have personal perceptions about what He can do in my life.**
   • **Am I willing to test my perceptions against the truth of His Word?**
   ○ **Yes** ○ **Not sure**

- **Am I willing to accept Jesus' teachings above my perceptions?**
  ○ Yes ○ Not sure
- **Am I willing to test what I have learned through experience and training in order to become like Jesus?** ○ Yes ○ Not sure

3. **If I were to grade myself (A=excellent; B=average; C=poor) on where I am in the process of being like Jesus, I would give myself a(n) _____ on denying self, a(n) _____ on putting my perceptions and preferences of Jesus on a cross, and a(n) _____ on following Him every day.**

4. **Do I understand that my true identity is found in my trust relationship of Jesus?** ○ Yes ○ Not sure

✛ **Record your feelings about today's study in your Identity Journal.**

DAY 3

JESUS SAID, "I AM!"

"I am the way and the truth and the life. No one comes to the Father except through me"
(John 14:6).

TODAY YOU WILL ...

○ write "I am" statements to describe yourself;
○ examine seven "I am" statements made by Jesus; and,
○ apply one of these statements to your relationship with Jesus.

I am a Christian. I am a husband and father. I am a pastor. I am a writer. I am a volunteer police and fire department chaplain. I am a conference leader, and I am a struggling, adopted child of God. This string of seven self-identifying statements is one way I can describe who I am to you. They tell you the different roles I serve as a person. Those roles make up part of my visible identity.

✠ **List seven titles in the margin that describe who you are. Be prepared to share your answers with your Identity Group.**

These statements tell others who you are by the roles you serve and the things you do. They are one way to tell others about yourself in order to help them understand you.

Jesus' "I Am" Statements

Jesus revealed who He was with seven self-identifying statements. These are not the only self-descriptive words of Jesus, but they will help you more fully answer the question, *Who is this Jesus?* The goal of your relationship with Jesus is to become like Him, and you cannot become like someone you do not know.

John, the disciple, recorded seven "I am" sayings of Jesus in the Book of John. Incidentally, do you know how God directed Moses to lead the people of Israel out of Egypt? Read *Exodus 3*. In God's call to Moses, God reveals His name to His servant. In *Exodus 3:13-17*, God revealed that His name is "I AM WHO I AM." God told Moses to tell Pharaoh and the people of Israel "I AM" sent him. God worked through Moses to free His people from bondage in Egypt.

This revelation of God's name is important to the "I am" sayings in John's Gospel. When Jesus said, "I am!" He was not only revealing things about Himself through the statements, He was associating Himself with the name of God! Jesus revealed He was God's Son by using the "I am" phrase. With that in mind, look at each of Jesus' statements that, in reality, begin with the name of God.

✠ **Read the following passages and match the Scripture with Jesus' identifying statement.**

John 6:35	The Gate
John 8:12; 9:5	The Resurrection and the Life
John 10:7,9	The True Vine
John 10:11	The Bread of Life
John 11:25	The Good Shepherd
John 14:6	The Light of the World
John 15:1,5	The Way, the Truth, the Life

The Bread of Life

Jesus fed 5,000 people in one sitting with only the contents of a boy's lunch. This got people's attention. They wanted to be one of His followers. Jesus, however, knew they were following because He filled their stomachs, not because He was their sustenance for life. So, Jesus stopped and told them He was not sent to fill their stomachs, but to be the bread of life *(John 6:35)*. Jesus said that just as God, "I AM," gave manna to sustain His people in the wilderness, God sent Jesus to be bread from heaven so that those who trust Him will never be hungry. Jesus promised that if they would accept Him as their daily source of life, He would give them eternal life *(John 6:40)*.

Then Jesus declared, "I am the bread of life. He who comes to me will never go hungry, and he who believes in me will never be thirsty" (John 6:35).

When Jesus spoke again to the people, he said, "I am the light of the world. Whoever follows me will never walk in darkness, but will have the light of life" (John 8:12).

"While I am in the world, I am the light of the world" (John 9:5).

Therefore Jesus said again, "I tell you the truth, I am the gate for the sheep" ... "I am the gate; whoever enters through me will be saved. He will come in and go out, and find pasture" (John 10:7,9).

> "I am the good shepherd. The good shepherd lays down his life for the sheep" (John 10:11).

> Jesus said to her, "I am the resurrection and the life. He who believes in me will live, even though he dies" (John 11:25).

> Jesus answered, "I am the way and the truth and the life. No one comes to the Father except through me" (John 14:6).

> "I am the true vide, and my father is the gardener." ... "I am the vine; you are the branches. If a man remains in me and I in him, he will bear much fruit; apart from me you can do nothing" (John 15:1,5).

The Light of the World

Jesus said "I am the light of the world" two times (John 8:12 and 9:5). The first time was before a group of religious leaders who challenged Jesus' witness to His claims. The religious leaders could not see God the Father as Jesus' witness (John 8:13-19). They needed divine light to know this truth. Jesus declared Himself to be the light of the world a second time when He was asked about a blind man's sin (John 9:1-5). Jesus taught His disciples that the man was not blind because he had sinned but so that the work of God might be displayed in his life.

The Gate

Jesus lived and taught in an agrarian society. Shepherds and sheep at that time were like cowboys and cattle in Texas at the end of the 19th century. Everyone in Jesus' day understood about farm and ranch life. Some people still do. Jesus often used analogies from common experiences to reveal who He was. One day Jesus must have been standing near a pen of sheep when he declared, "I am the gate for the sheep" (John 10:7). Jesus taught He was the entrance to safety, provision, and care. Sheep outside the pen were vulnerable to predators. But inside the pen, under the care and protection of the shepherd, they were safe. Jesus promised that those who sought safety and care and entered through Him would be saved (John 10:9).

The Good Shepherd

In the same setting Jesus declared, "I am the good shepherd" (John 10:11). Once inside the pen, sheep still need someone to stand by the entrance to protect them. Sheep need a shepherd to guide and care for them, too. Jesus said He was the good shepherd who "lays down his life for the sheep" (John 10:11). Hired hands run at the sign of danger. But true shepherds risk their lives for the sheep. Good shepherds also know the names of their sheep, and the sheep know their shepherd (John 10:14). Jesus was foretelling His death, burial, and resurrection when He described Himself this way.

The Resurrection and the Life

Lazarus, Mary, and Martha were friends of Jesus. Lazarus died, and Jesus waited four days until He came to Bethany to see the family. When Martha declared that if Jesus had been present her brother would not have died, Jesus promised Lazarus would rise again (John 11:23). Martha said she knew he would be raised at the last day. Jesus looked into her tear-filled eyes and said, "I am the resurrection and the life" (John 11:25). Jesus continued, "He who believes in me will live, even though he dies; and whoever lives and believes in me will never die" (John 11:25-26). Martha and the family had missed the fact that Jesus was "I am" who would raise those who believed from the grave and give them eternal life. Jesus called Lazarus from the grave. Jesus' friend came out, and the people believed in Jesus (John 11:45).

The Way, the Truth, and the Life

Jesus' closest disciples were concerned. He had been talking a lot about His death. They had seen things turn sour over their last week together in Jerusalem. Jesus gathered them together and promised them a place in heaven. He was going to prepare them a place, and if they would trust Him, He would return and take them there. Jesus said they knew the way to where He was headed. Thomas, the doubter, missed Jesus' point and asked, *"Lord, we don't know where you are going, so how can we know the way?" (John 14:5).* (Jesus wants to hear this from you before He can help you.) Jesus answered Thomas, *"I am the way and the truth and the life. No one comes to the Father except through me" (John 14:6).* Jesus said that if anyone would follow Him, they would know the way to heaven.

The True Vine

In His last days with His disciples, Jesus gave them another picture of His identity and their relationship with Him. Who Jesus is determines how people relate to Him. Walking along a path outlined in grapevines, Jesus stopped and pointed to the vines. Jesus said, *"I am the true vine, and my Father is the gardener" (John 15:1).* Jesus went on to say, *"I am the vine; you are the branches" (John 15:5).* Jesus identified Himself as the source of life for His followers, and explained that their relationship with Him was to be as close and dependent as the vine and branches. This analogy is the basis for how a follower of Jesus becomes like Jesus and how His disciples find the nurturing resources to live for Him.

What Do These Mean to You?

Here are some ways these seven pictures can help you answer the question, "Who is this Jesus?"

- The Bread of Life: Jesus is your source of daily strength for living.
- The Light of the World: Jesus is how you see in a dark world of sin.
- The Gate: A relationship with Jesus is how you enter a relationship with God.
- The Good Shepherd: Jesus cares for, guides, and protects you.
- The Resurrection and the Life: Jesus is your hope for eternal life and the promise you will be raised to life after your physical death.
- The Way, the Truth, and the Life: Jesus is the only way to heaven, the truth by which you make decisions, and your source of life.
- The True Vine: Jesus is your source of spiritual life, and you are dependent upon Him to produce God's fruit in your life.

SUMMARY

- Your "I am" statements describe in part who you are to others.
- Jesus revealed who He was by His seven "I am" statements.
- By using "I am," Jesus revealed He was the Son of God.
- Jesus' statements about His identity are the basis of how you relate to Him.

PERSONAL REFLECTION

✚ **Prayerfully complete these activities in your Identity Journal.**

1. The seven self-identifying statements by Jesus reveal who He is and how He wants to relate to you. Briefly explain which analogy touched your heart most and why.
2. The goal of the Christian life is to be like Jesus. How does the image of Jesus as the true vine help you obtain that goal?
3. Jesus described Himself as the Good Shepherd. What understanding does this image give you about Jesus?

DAY 4

THE NAME ABOVE ALL NAMES

"God highly exalted Him, and bestowed on Him the name which is above every name" *(Phil. 2:9, NASB).*

TODAY YOU WILL ...

○ prepare the story of your name for your Identity Group;
○ examine the names given to Jesus by the prophets and Mary prior to His birth;
○ examine biblical names and phrases of Jesus that describe His identity; and,
○ write your personal confession of the true identity of Jesus.

Your name is important. In many ways, it is your identity. Your name tells who you are; and names others give you make a difference in how you perceive yourself. For example, my full name is Carl Gene Wilkes.

My father's first name is Carl, and my mother's middle name is Jean. So, when they had their first son, they gave me their names. My name reminds me whose I am as well as who I am.

✚ **Do you know why you were given your name or why your friends have given you a nickname? What does that information tell you about who you are? Write the story behind your name or nickname. Be prepared to share it in your Identity Group.**

_____

_____

_____

_____

_____

Names of Jesus Before and at His Birth

Jesus was given names, too. Each portrays some aspect of His work as God's Son. God, the Father, desired that His Son's names tell the roles He would fulfill to reveal God's eternal purposes. Long before Jesus came to live and serve among people, prophets of God told of Jesus' coming. They used names and titles that told of His true identity. Isaiah, one of God's prophets, lived over seven hundred years before the birth of Jesus.

✚ **Read Isaiah 9:6. Underline the names of the child who would be born to Israel.**

Isaiah proclaimed God's Promised Child would have the names *Wonderful Counselor, Mighty God, Everlasting Father, and Prince of Peace*. Each of these names tells us about the true identity of Jesus. Counselor was also the name of Jesus' promised Holy Spirit *(John 14:16)*. Jesus was preexistent with God, the Father *(John 1:1-3)*. New Testament writers tell us *"He ... is our peace" (Eph. 2:14)*.

God's prophet Zechariah wrote that *"The Lord will be king over all the earth; in that day the Lord will be the only one, and His name the only one" (Zech. 14:9, NASB)*. Jesus would be the king over all the earth, not just the nation of Israel.

When all things were right according to God's eternal plan, Jesus was born. An angel came to Mary before the birth of her first son and told her to name Him Jesus, *"He will save His people from their sins" (Matt. 1:21, NASB)*. The angel said this was to fulfill the prophecy that His name be "Immanuel," which translated means, *"God with us" (Matt. 1:23, NASB)*. God's chosen name for His son tells all people that He came to save. Immanuel supports the biblical teaching of Jesus as God coming in the form of a human. (See *Phil. 2:5-11*.)

Names of Jesus After His Return to Heaven

After the birth, life, death, burial, and resurrection of Jesus, God chose writers to teach about the identity of Jesus. One of those writers, Paul, knew the meaning of Jesus' given name and used the name *Savior*

> *To us a child is born, to us a son is given, and the government will be on his shoulders. And he will be called Wonderful Counselor, Mighty God, Everlasting Father, Prince of Peace (Isa. 9:6).*

> *He is the image of the invisible God, the firstborn over all creation. For by him all things were created: things in heaven and on earth, visible and invisible, whether thrones or powers or rulers or authorities; all things were created by him and for him. He is before all things, and in him all things hold together. And he is the head of the body, the church; he is the beginning and the firstborn from among the dead, so that in everything he might have the supremacy* (Col. 1:15-18).

----

throughout his letters to the churches. (See *Titus 1:4; 2:13; 3:6.*) Other books in the Bible use the full title and name of Jesus, the Lord Jesus Christ (for example, *Rom. 1:7*).

Paul wrote a letter to the church in Colossae to explain the identity of Jesus. This town was like many cities today—cosmopolitan with diverse religious and cultural elements. Paul wanted to clarify any misunderstanding of who Jesus was to the new Christians there.

⊕ **Read Colossians 1:15-18. Then write in the margin phrases from these verses that describe Jesus.**

Creator and Sustainer of All Things

While these are not names of Jesus, each one tells about what He does as the Son of God. Jesus is *"the image of the invisible God" (Col. 1:15a).* To see Jesus is to see the full character and person of God. To know Jesus is to know God. Jesus is the *"firstborn over all creation"* and *"by him all things were created" (Col. 1:15b-16).* Jesus was preexistent before creation, and He is the creator of all things that exist, both physical and spiritual. Jesus is *"before all things, and in him all things hold together" (Col. 1:17).* Jesus not only existed as God before reality as we know it, but His very presence holds all things together.

Let me make this last phrase real to you. Scientists have learned that energy is the basic building block of all things. You may know Albert Einstein's explanation of physical reality that led us into the atomic age: $E=MC^2$. Energy holds the smallest units of matter together, and those units compose the physical universe. If you trust the Word of God, this energy has a name. Its name is Jesus! In Him all things hold together! In a prescientific world God revealed who Jesus was for ages to come. In this world of electron microscopes and quantum theory we can experience the truth of this ancient description of Jesus by accepting by faith that Jesus is the very energy that holds reality together. Remove the energy (Jesus) and you will see the collapse of the physical universe. (See *2 Pet. 3:10.*) This also can help us understand the chaos that will be brought on creation when Jesus removes Himself in the end times!

More Names for Jesus

The Bible also calls Jesus, *"the head of the body, the church" (Col. 1:18).* This description tells us Jesus is supreme not only over all creation but also over those who enter into a personal relationship with Him. Jesus is *"the firstborn from among the dead" (Col. 1:18).* The resurrection of Jesus signaled a new order in creation. Jesus not only created all things, He is the first of a new order of creation—those who will experience eternal life through a relationship with Jesus.

God inspired other writers to use special names for Jesus that allow us to see the breadth and depth of who He really is.

A name for Jesus is the *"Word" (John 1:1,14).* God inspired John, a disciple of Jesus, to equate Jesus with the important ancient concept of the word. In the Old Testament, God spoke through many prophets and kings. Isaiah spoke God's words to Israel by beginning his message with the phrase, *"This is what the Lord says" (Isa. 45:1)* or, *"Thus saith the Lord"* (KJV). This told the listeners that what they were about to hear was God's message, not that of the prophet. By calling Jesus *"the Word,"* John teaches us that Jesus is the ultimate and final word spoken by God. Jesus is the only voice you need to hear to have a right relationship with God.

John also names Jesus the *"advocate" (1 John 2:1,* KJV). This word has also been translated as *"one who speaks to the Father in our defense."* This name of Jesus teaches us that when we sin, Jesus stands before the throne of God, the Father, like a defense attorney pleading our case.

Names of Jesus in the Revelation of John

Revelation is the final book of the Bible. Its message is one of hope—the God who began all things is the same God who will bring all things to an end. This book of prophecy gives us a glimpse of eternity. It portrays Jesus in His exalted state as the reigning, resurrected Savior. One name of Jesus revealed to John is the Lion of the tribe of Judah *(Rev. 5:5).* This title is a fulfillment of God's promise to bring an eternal king to the throne of David who was from the tribe of Judah.

Jesus is also called *"the Alpha and the Omega" (Rev. 1:8; 22:13), "the First and the Last" (Rev. 1:17),* and *"the Beginning and the End" (Rev. 21:6; 22:13).* Jesus created all things as we know them, and He will bring them all to completion.

One of the most used names of Jesus in Revelation is *"the Lamb"* (for example, *Rev. 5:8,12-13).* The name teaches us that Jesus was and is the final sacrifice that brought atonement for all people. Like the blood of the Passover lamb in the Old Testament (see *Ex. 12),* Jesus' sacrificial blood covers the sin of anyone who trusts Him. The apostle Paul called Jesus *"our Passover lamb"* who *"has been sacrificed"* for us *(1 Cor. 5:7).* After His death, Jesus was resurrected and exalted to the right hand of the Father. His name, the Lamb, signifies His sacrifice and love for those He came to save. To call Jesus the Lamb of God is to tell the story of His death, burial, and resurrection.

What's in a Name?

I told you my father's name is Carl. Growing up, his nickname was *Corky.* When I was a boy, we would go back to his hometown of Happy (I am not making this up!) in the panhandle of Texas. There I was "Corky's boy." After getting over the embarrassment of holding such a title, I began to ask people about Corky. As they told me stories of my father's childhood and teenage years, I gained a whole new appreciation for the man I called my father.

You may only have known the Son of God by the name Jesus. Today, you have learned other names for Him. If you will sit down and read the stories behind those names, you will gain a new appreciation for the One you call Lord and Savior. Your relationship with Him will grow as you learn to relate to Him in the many ways He reveals Himself.

SUMMARY

- God revealed Jesus' coming through prophets who used several names to reveal what Jesus would do as God's Son.
- Jesus is the Creator and Sustainer of all things. He is the image of the invisible God and the first to be resurrected to eternal life.
- God inspired writers of the New Testament to use names to describe His work as the Son of God.
- Knowing the names and descriptions of Jesus will deepen your relationship with Him.

PERSONAL REFLECTION

Prayerfully complete these activities in your Identity Journal.

1. **Consider the names Jesus and Immanuel. What do they tell you about who Jesus is and what He came to do?**
2. **Write the name of Jesus that touched your heart most in today's study. Explain why it struck you the way it did. Be prepared to share your answers with your Identity Group.**
3. **God revealed to John the name "The Lamb." What does that name tell you about Jesus? Could you explain its significance?**

DAY 5

TRUSTING THE JESUS YOU KNOW

"On that day you will realize that I am in my Father, and you are in me, and I am in you" (John 14:20).

TODAY YOU WILL ...

○ recall a personal name that has special meaning;
○ examine the biblical doctrine of the Trinity;
○ examine the biblical phrase "in Christ";
○ be given an opportunity to become "in Christ" and enjoy the benefits of that relationship; and,
○ write a prayer inviting God to be the source of your true identity.

I have two daughters. They learned my given name because I taught it to them as they learned to talk. As the oldest entered her teenage years, she would occasionally call me by my given name. I let it slide the first two or three times, but the next time I stopped her and said, "You are getting old enough to call me by my given name, but, you know what, only two girls on this planet can call me daddy. Everyone else calls me Gene. I would be honored if you called me daddy instead of Gene." She thought for a minute and said, "OK, Daddy" and walked off. She's 17 now and calls me dad. I'm honored when she calls me by that name.

⊕ **What are some names that are special to you? Write one of those names and the meaning it has for you in the margin. Plan to share that name and its meaning with your Identity Group.**

Names can be simply ways to get people's attention. They can also be ways to honor those whose names you call. You have examined many of the names of Jesus, and you may have found new meaning in your relationship with Him through knowing these names. But, studying the names of Jesus does not mean you have a relationship with Him. Without trusting Jesus, you can only call His name and never know the intimacy of having a living relationship with Him.

Jesus said, "I Am in the Father."

One day, Philip, a disciple of Jesus, said, *"Lord, show us the Father and that will be enough for us [to trust you]" (John 14:8)*. Philip was like you and me. We want to make sure Jesus is really God. If we could just see God and Jesus together, we know we would trust Him. Jesus' reply to Philip was, *" 'Anyone who has seen me has seen the Father. ... Don't you believe that I am in the Father, and that the Father is in me?' " (John 14:9-10)*. Jesus declared that to know Him is to know God, the Father.

Let's consider an important biblical doctrine, the Trinity. This is important because if your true identity is in a relationship with Jesus, you must fully know who Jesus is. Jesus taught that He and God, the Father, are one *(John 14:10)*. Remember that the Bible teaches that Jesus was preexistent as God. It also teaches that upon His ascension into heaven, Jesus sent another Counselor, the Holy Spirit *(John 14:16; see also Acts 2)*. These passages are among many that teach us that God is three-in-one. God, "I AM," is Father, Son, and Holy Spirit. To know and experience any person of the Trinity is to know and experience all three Persons. Allow me to explain it this way: I am one person, but I relate to different people as father, son, and friend. I am always the same person, but my relationship with people reveals different ways of being me with each one. The three-in-one Person of God relates to us the same way.

And You Are "in Christ"

Jesus affirmed His unity with God, the Father, but He added that you are in unity with Him if you trust and obey Him. Jesus said, *" 'I am in my Father, and you are in me, and I am in you' " (John 14:20)*. It is a deep mystery how we are actually "in Christ," but Jesus said we are in a relationship with Him like He is in His Father. The Bible describes our relationship with God through faith in Jesus as being "in Christ." It is another way of understanding Jesus' words that "you are in me." Let's look at some of the "in Christ" passages to see what it means to have a relationship with Jesus.

⊕ **Read the following passages and write what each teaches about being "in Christ."**

Romans 6:11 _____

Romans 6:23 _____

Romans 8:1 _____

Ephesians 1:7 _____

Ephesians 1:11 _____

In the same way, count yourselves dead to sin but alive to God in Christ Jesus (Rom. 6:11).

The wages of sin is death, but the gift of God is eternal life in Christ Jesus our Lord (Rom. 6:23).

Therefore, there is now no condemnation for those who are in Christ Jesus (Rom. 8:1).

In him we have redemption through his blood, the forgiveness of sins, in accordance with the riches of God's grace (Eph. 1:7).

In him we were also chosen, having been predestined according to the plan of him who works out everything in conformity with the purpose of his will (Eph. 1:11).

"In Christ" means you are dead to the influence of sin and alive toward the things of God. (See *Rom. 6:11*.) You have eternal life when you are in Christ *(Rom. 6:23)*. The Bible says there is no condemnation if you are in Christ *(Rom. 8:1)*. You have salvation and forgiveness of sin "in Him" *(Eph. 1:7)*. In your relationship with Jesus through faith you were chosen according to God's purposes. (See *Eph. 1:11*.)

Being "in Christ" is one way to describe your spiritual identity to others. It means you have come to the place in your life where the most important relationship that defines who you are is your relationship with Jesus.

Are You "in Christ"?

As we complete this week's study of Jesus, we should not go any further without making sure you know for certain your identity rests in Christ. You may have allowed other things in your life to define your identity. You may have only known the name or names of Jesus but never entered into a faith relationship with Him. Take a moment to pause and confirm your identity with Christ.

How do you know if you are "in Christ"? Let's start with Jesus' words. Just after He told His disciples " 'I am in you,' " Jesus said, " 'Whoever has my commands and obeys them, he is the one who loves me. He who loves me will be loved by my Father, and I too will love him and show myself to him'" (John 14:20-21).

Jesus said we are in Him when we obey His commands. This is how we show our love for Him. (See *John 15:9-10*.) Paul wrote to the Ephesians that you become "in Christ" by hearing and trusting the word of truth. (See *Eph. 1:13*.) The crux of the identity matter is obeying Jesus and trusting the truth of God's Word. How do you obey, and what is the word of truth?

God's Word says, *"the wages of sin is death"* (Rom. 6:23). In other words, the earned consequences of living in sin is death without God. But, the gift of God is eternal life in Christ Jesus our Lord *(Rom. 6:23)*. God offers you the gift of forgiveness of sin and eternal life through trusting that Jesus died, was buried, and rose on the third day.

Your decision today is whether to trust that Jesus is who He said He is and thus experience a relationship with Him. You can be "in Christ" by sincerely praying this prayer:

> *Dear God, I know that Jesus is Your Son and that He died and was raised from the dead. Because I have sinned and need forgiveness, I ask Jesus to save me. I am willing to change the direction of my life by acknowledging Jesus as my Savior and Lord and by turning away from my sins. Thank you for giving me forgiveness, eternal life, and hope. In Jesus' name. Amen.*

✦ **You may have already prayed this prayer and are confident you are "in Christ." Or you may not have fully grasped what that relationship had to do with your identity and how you live your life. If this is true for you, in the margin, write a prayer to God**

Dear God, _____

_____
_____
_____
_____
_____
_____
_____
_____
_____
_____
_____
_____
_____
_____

asking forgiveness for allowing others and your own thinking to confuse your understanding of your identity in Him. Ask God to show you how to rest in Whose you are as well as who you are.

SUMMARY

- Jesus, the Father, and the Holy Spirit are three persons, one God.
- You are "in Christ" as Jesus is one with the Father. This is a mystery accepted by faith.
- You can have the peace of eternal life by putting your trust in Christ.
- Your true identity is knowing the truths of being "in Christ."

PERSONAL REFLECTION

⊕ **Prayerfully complete these activities in your Identity Journal.**

The thought of genuinely being "in Christ" means that ...
1. I ○ have ○ have not confessed that people and events have defined my identity, and I ○ have ○ have not asked Jesus to be my true identity.
2. I ○ have ○ have not confessed my sins and accepted God's free gift of salvation in Christ Jesus.
3. I can truthfully say that I ○ am ○ am not living every day with the confidence and knowledge of who I am in Christ.

WEEK 2
A NEW IDENTITY: YOUR CALL

This week you will ...
- observe how your response to God's call on your life is the single, most transforming event in your life—all else flows from it (Day 1);
- learn from Moses' experience when he resisted but eventually accepted God's call on his life (Day 2);
- examine how God called Saul to take the good news of Jesus to all peoples, and learn five lessons from God's encounter with Saul (Day 3);
- the distortion of separating calling from career and learn how call affects every aspect of your life (Day 4); and,
- review the biblical passages that teach that the appropriate response to God's call is to trust and obey (Day 5).

Memory Verse:
"I urge you to live a life worthy of the calling you have received" (Eph. 4:1).

The "Call of God" may seem like something from a long, boring sermon or a bad Hollywood film about spiritual themes. But it's actually how God comes to you and invites you to become "in Christ." God comes to you and calls you to become like Jesus and to join Him in accomplishing His purposes on earth. This invitation (call) changes everything about your life—if you say yes to God's call.

When Jesus began His public ministry He did not encourage people to *be all you can be.* He told them to follow Him and they would enter the kingdom of heaven. He did not invite them to lead with Him, Jesus called people to follow Him. Some followed. Others turned away. Their decision determined how they lived the rest of their lives. It determined their eternal destiny. Jesus specifically called twelve men to be His closest disciples. That call changed every aspect of their lives.

This week you will examine God's call on His closest followers' lives as well as His call on your life. Your response to God's call to follow Him will be as significant as your decision to agree with God that Jesus is the Son of God. Why? Your response to God's call on your life is the single most transforming event in your life—all else flows from it. Your answer to Jesus' question, "Who do you say I am?" establishes your relationship with God through faith. Your response to Jesus' call to follow Him will determine how you live your life and will become the context for your becoming like Jesus.

DAY 1

FOLLOW ME

"Come, follow me, ... and I will make you fishers of men" (Matt. 4:19).

TODAY YOU WILL ...

○ research the New Testament concept of being a disciple;
○ review Jesus' call to certain people to follow Him;
○ examine the difference Jesus' call made in the lives of those who followed Him; and,
○ determine your response to God's call to follow Him.

You have learned everything of importance from someone else. Very few people are self-taught. Everyone learns how to walk, talk, and treat others from someone else.

⊕ **Identify in the margin three or four people who have taught you an important skill or provided you with some wisdom for how to live your life. List the person's name and what you learned from him or her. For example, I learned how to talk from my parents. I learned to read Greek from my college professor, Dr. Cutter. Be prepared to share your list in your Identity Group.**

You were a student of those who taught you the basic as well as the complicated things of life. They taught by example and by words. You followed their examples and became like them in some way or another. Their influence is partially why you live the way you do now. Learning from others is the simplest form of discipleship.

No Word for Discipleship

If you were to search a Bible concordance for the word *discipleship*, you would not find it. You would find *disciple, disciples,* and *discipline,* but not *discipleship.* We have coined it to describe all aspects of being a follower

---

People who have taught me: _____
_____
_____
_____
_____
_____
_____
_____

of Jesus. A disciple in Jesus' day was someone who committed himself to learn from a teacher. Generally, there were no schools as there are today. People learned by literally following the teacher wherever he led. Learning in Jesus' day was not just the transfer of information, but the adoption of a way of life. When Jesus called people, He was calling them to arrange everything about their lives in order to follow Him.

To be a disciple is more like being an apprentice than being a student. Dallas Willard said it this way, "If I am Jesus' disciple that means I am with him to learn from him how to be like him."[1] The goal of following Jesus is to become like Jesus, not simply to learn facts from Him.

A follower relationship with Jesus begins with a call. Jesus calls or summons you to be His disciple and to become like Him. If you accept His call, you become His follower. Here's my working definition of a disciple: *A disciple is an ordinary person who trusts that Jesus is the Son of God and follows Him.* This description of a disciple finds its beginning in Jesus' call to invite you to join Him as an apprentice of how to live life His way.

Ordinary People Who Follow Jesus

✠ **What do you know about those who followed Jesus? What are your impressions of them? Place a check beside the phrase that best describes your feelings about those whom Jesus first called to follow Him.**
- ○ **exceptional people who easily grasped the things of God**
- ○ **ordinary people who were a lot like me**
- ○ **people who are clueless to the things of God until Jesus called them to follow Him**
- ○ **simple, quiet people whom Jesus transformed into mighty people of God**

✠ **Let's take a look at what the first followers of Jesus looked like. Read Matthew 4:18-22.**
Who did Jesus call and what were their professions? _____
_____
_____

What did Jesus call them to do? How did they respond? _____
_____
_____
_____

Jesus was walking beside the Sea of Galilee when He spotted Peter and his brother Andrew fishing. They were commercial fishermen. Jesus said, *"Come, follow me, ... and I will make you fishers of men."* They dropped what they were doing and followed Him. A little farther down the shore, Jesus saw James and John, brothers who owned a fishing company, mending their nets. Jesus called them and they immediately left what they were doing. A call. Then a response. Life would never be the same for these ordinary people.

> *A disciple is an ordinary person who trusts that Jesus is the Son of God and follows Him.*

> *As Jesus was walking beside the Sea of Galilee, he saw two brothers, Simon called Peter and his brother Andrew. They were casting a net into the lake, for they were fishermen. "Come, follow me," Jesus said, "and I will make you fishers of men." At once they left their nets and followed him. Going on from there, he saw two other brothers, James son of Zebedee and his brother John. They were in a boat with their father Zebedee, preparing their nets. Jesus called them, and immediately they left the boat and their father and followed him (Matt. 4:18-22).*

The Call

Jesus called them to stop fishing for fish so He could make them fishers of people. He meant, I will make you people fishermen, not I will give you a lesson on how to bait, catch, and fillet others. Jesus' call was one of transformation of lifestyle, not simply of joining Him in a psychology or sociology class.

✦ **Read Matthew 9:9-13.**

Whom did Jesus call and what was his profession? _____

_____

How did this person respond to Jesus? _____

_____

_____

What did Matthew do the evening Jesus called him? _____

_____

_____

Who didn't like Jesus hanging around with sinners? _____

_____

_____

What was Jesus' response? _____

_____

_____

Jesus continued to call people to follow Him. One day He passed a booth where a man named Matthew sat collecting taxes for the Roman government. Jesus told Matthew to follow Him, and he did. That night Matthew threw a party for his friends so they could see Jesus. Some religious leaders showed up and began to criticize Jesus for hanging out with sinners. Jesus' responded, *"It is not the healthy who need a doctor, but the sick."*

Jesus called these and others to follow Him, to learn a way of life from Him, and to enter the kingdom of heaven with Him. Jesus' call to follow was the single most important event in their lives. Their decision to deny everything they were doing and had done to follow Jesus was the single most important decision they made in their lives.

✦ **Imagine Jesus standing in front of you saying, "Follow me!"**
   What would your response be? Check your answer below.
   ○ **Let's go!**
   ○ **Let me think about it.**
   ○ **Can I bring along all my stuff?**
   ○ **Where are you taking me?**
   ○ **Wow! I can't believe you want me to follow You!**
   ○ **You've got to be kidding. I've got work to do.**

Your response may be similar to or different from those listed, but whatever it is, it will determine how you live the rest of your life. You may have been a Christian for many years, but you just realized the impact of Jesus' call on your life. Stop now and consider all it means to respond to Jesus' call to *"deny [yourself] and take up [your] cross daily and follow me" (Luke 9:23).*

Your salvation is secure if you have trusted Jesus as the Christ and accepted in faith His forgiveness. But, you may not know the presence of God in your life. You may be wondering why you live with the same habits and defeats you've had all your life. The answer may be your refusal to follow Jesus closely enough to be changed into His likeness.

SUMMARY

• You have learned the most important things in life from someone else.
• Jesus called people to follow Him, not to sign up for a class.
• The goal of following Jesus is to adopt His lifestyle.
• Jesus chose ordinary people like you to follow Him.
• A person's response to Jesus' call is the most transforming event in his or her life.

PERSONAL REFLECTION

⊕ **Prayerfully complete these activities in your Identity Journal.**

1. **When you first read about Peter, Andrew, James, and John's immediate responses to follow Jesus, what did you think?**
2. **How do you respond to Dallas Willard's statement, "If I am Jesus' disciple that means I am with him to learn from him how to be like him."**
3. **In what ways are you like the first people Jesus called to follow Him? In what ways are you different?**
4. **React to this statement: Your response to God's call on your life is the single, most transforming event in your life–all else flows from it.**
5. **Make a list of implications for your life if you were to get up and follow Jesus as Matthew and the others did. How would that affect your job, family, and church life?**

> Your response to God's call is the most transforming event in your life— all else flows from it.

[1]Dallas Willard, *The Divine Conspiracy* (San Francisco: HarperCollins, 1998), 276.

DAY 2

WHO ME?

"Who am I, that I should go?"
(Ex. 3:11).—Moses

TODAY YOU WILL ...

○ Learn about a person who did not follow Jesus' call;
○ examine the concept of a "crisis of belief";
○ observe how Moses responded to God's call to work through him; and,
○ review five questions of resistance and God's responses.

Not everyone was as willing to follow Jesus as His first disciples. You may remember the story of the rich young man who came to Jesus and asked, *"what must I do to inherit eternal life?" (Mark 10:17).* After Jesus perceived that the man had put his faith in keeping the commandments and in what he acquired, Jesus called him to *"sell everything you have and give to the poor, and you will have treasure in heaven" (v. 21).*

✜ **Read Mark 10:17-22. List two or three reasons you believe the rich young man and others like him refuse to do what Jesus calls them to do.** _____

_____

_____

_____

_____

_____

Jesus' call was a decision point in the young man's life. The Bible says he walked away from Jesus because he was very rich. Selling his possessions would have made him trust in Jesus alone. Following Jesus means risking everything earthly to acquire something heavenly. This young man did not want to take the risk.

> As Jesus started on his way, a man ran up to him and fell on his knees before him. "Good teacher," he asked, "what must I do to inherit eternal life?" "Why do you call me good?" Jesus answered. "No one is good—except God alone. You know the commandments: 'Do not murder, do not commit adultery, do not steal, do not give false testimony, do not defraud, honor your father and mother.' " "Teacher," he declared, "all these I have kept since I was a boy." Jesus looked at him and loved him. "One thing you lack," he said. "Go, sell everything you have and give to the poor, and you will have treasure in heaven. Then come, follow me." At this the man's face fell. He went away sad, because he had great wealth (Mark 10:17-22).

A Decision to Follow

God called Moses to lead His people out of Egypt. Their conversation at the burning bush reveals five ways we may question the call of God on our lives and five answers God gives in response. Turn to *Exodus 3* and *4* in your Bible.

✦ **Read Exodus 3:10. What was God's call to Moses?** _____
_____
_____
_____

✦ **Read Exodus 3:11. What was Moses' statement to God?** _____
_____
_____

✦ **Read Exodus 3:12. What was God's response to Moses?** _____
_____
_____
_____

God came to Moses in a burning bush and called him to go to Pharaoh and bring His people out of Egypt. Moses had grown up and worked in Egypt. He knew what a job that would be. Moses' first response to God is what I call the question of **adequacy**. Moses asked, *"Who am I, that I should go?"* Many times our first response to God's call is, Who me? We think we are not adequate to do something for God.

God doesn't see things the same way we do. God has an eternal perspective on history. When God calls a person to join Him, God knows the why and how of His choice. God did not accept Moses' answer. **God's presence** was His answer to Moses' question of adequacy. When Moses asked, "Who am I?" God answered, *"It doesn't matter who you are. I will be with you. That is all that matters."*

> **Many times our first response to God's call is, Who me?**

✦ **Read Exodus 3:13. What was Moses' second question to God?**
_____
_____
_____

✦ **Read Exodus 3:14-15. What was God's response?** _____
_____
_____

Moses' next question was the question of **authority**. When God calls you to go into a possible hostile audience, you want them to know who sent you. Moses wanted to know what to say if asked, *"What is his name [who sent you]?"* Moses was concerned that his own people would not believe him because he had killed an Egyptian. He asked God by what authority he could justify his actions. **God's name** was the answer. God revealed His name to Moses when He said, *"I am who I* *am ... I am has sent me to you" (Ex. 3:14).* God let Moses know His authority came not from who Moses was, but who God was.

✣ **Read Exodus 4:1. What was Moses' third question to God?**

_____

_____

✣ **Read Exodus 4:2-9. What was God's response to Moses?** ____

_____

_____

_____

Moses asked the question of **authenticity** when he asked God, *"What if they do not believe me or listen to me?" (Ex. 4:1).* Moses did not fear Pharaoh's response as much as he did his own people's response! He knew what the king of Egypt would say. But, what about those he had to lead after Pharaoh agreed to let the Israelites go? We want to prove that God is the author of our actions and that He is real to those God calls us to lead. We fear God's call is not enough to see us through.

God answered Moses by demonstrating His **presence** in Moses' life. God gave Moses three visible signs that He was supernaturally working in his life. He changed a staff into a snake and back again. God's work in our lives is His answer to our question of authenticity. Past experiences with the living God remind us of His power and presence in our lives. God is real to others when He is real in our lives.

> **We want to prove that God is the author of our actions and that He is real to those God calls us to lead.**

> **God is real to others when He is real in our lives.**

✣ **Read Exodus 4:10. What did Moses say to God next?** _____

_____

✣ **Read Exodus 4:12. What was God's response?** _____

_____

_____

_____

Moses complained to God that this was a speaking job, and that he had never been an eloquent speaker. He was too slow a thinker and stuttered in pressure situations. Moses begged the question of **ability** when he said he could not speak well. God would not accept that excuse. God asked a series of rhetorical questions that all implied **God's word** was the answer to Moses' question of ability. God said that He made Moses' mouth, and He would make it work if God needed it to work! God's word was more powerful than Moses' ability. So, it didn't matter if Moses was mute. God's word was the power, not Moses' ability.

✣ **Read Exodus 4:13. What was Moses' next resisting comment to God?** _____

_____

_____

✦ **Read Exodus 4:14-17. How did God respond to Moses?** _____
_____
_____

Moses ran out of reasons that he couldn't accept God's call. So, he resorted to begging God to send someone else. This is what I call the question of audacity. Moses had the **audacity** to question God's plan for his life and to suggest that God could do a better job of asking whom He sent! According to Moses, God had the wrong guy! The Bible said that God's anger burned against Moses. But, God's patience overcame God's anger. His answer to Moses' question of audacity was **God's provision** of a partner in ministry. God said Moses' brother Aaron would accompany him to visit Pharaoh. Moses could no longer resist God's call on his life. He returned from the burning bush encounter with God, and his life was never the same.

Your Questions and God's Answers

God may not have appeared to you in a burning bush, but God has revealed Himself in Jesus, the Bible, prayer, and His Holy Spirit. God has called you to a saving relationship with Him and to live for and like Him. Like Moses, you have a choice to accept, resist, or deny that call.

What do you believe God has called you to do for Him? Don't overlook God's call to salvation. Don't overlook Jesus' call to every Christian to make disciples of all ethnic groups *(Matt. 28:19)*.

✦ **Write a brief summary of what you believe God has called you to do. (Example: God wants me to go to my neighbor and share with her the good news of salvation.)**_____
_____
_____
_____
_____
_____
_____
_____
_____

✦ **Go back through this lesson about Moses. Make a list of the questions of resistance and God's answers to them in the spaces below. They are identified in bold type in each section.**
○ **Question of _____. God's _____ is the answer.**
○ **Question of _____. God's _____ is the answer.**
○ **Question of _____. God's _____ is the answer.**
○ **Question of _____. God's _____ is the answer.**
○ **Question of _____. God's _____ is the answer.**

Now go back through the list and place a check beside the question of resistance with which you most identify. Relate that question to what you trust God has called you to do. Be prepared to share your answer and the reason for your choice with your Identity Group.

SUMMARY

- Not everyone responds positively to Jesus' call to follow Him.
- God's "invitation for you to work with Him" creates a crisis point in which you must decide to follow that call or live as usual.
- Moses' conversation with God at the burning bush reveals five ways we question the call of God and five answers God gives in response.
- God has called you to a saving relationship with Him and to live for and like Him. You have a choice to accept, resist, or deny that call.

PERSONAL REFLECTION

✙ **Prayerfully complete these activities in your Identity Journal.**

1. **In what ways are you like the rich, young man who came to Jesus? Have you asked the question of eternal life? Have you tried to justify your current lifestyle rather than follow Jesus? What in your life is keeping you from accepting Jesus' call?**
2. **Describe a personal "crisis of belief."**
3. **In what ways are you like Moses in his response to God's call? How did his questions affect you? What did they reveal about your faith in God?**
4. **If you have already said yes to God's call on your life, what changes have you made in order to do what God has called you to do?**
5. **If you were to say yes to God's call, what changes do you foresee?**

DAY 3

YES, YOU!

"This man is my chosen instrument to carry my name before the Gentiles and their kings and before the people of Israel" (Acts 9:15).

TODAY YOU WILL ...

○ read how one person's response to God's call changed how he lived his life;
○ examine the biblical account of God's call to Saul of Tarsus to carry the good news of Jesus to the entire world; and,
○ review some lessons you can learn from Saul's response to God.

I had been a youth minister for three years and working with students for seven years when the call came. A friend asked me to join him working for a private foundation that ran youth camps year-round. I had never considered serving God in such a way. I had only known being on a church staff as the way to respond to God's call on my life. What would such a change mean to my "career"? I was at a big church. Why would I leave that situation to serve in an unknown foundation? After much prayer with my wife and others, we decided to leave the church staff position and serve God through this camping ministry. Our response to that call changed the course of our lives forever. Oddly enough, that decision to follow what we believed to be God's specific call at the time was the bridge that led to my place of service as a pastor today. But, that is another story.

That experience caused me to answer God's call to use all He has made me to be and all He has given me to do His will. I stood like Moses in front of the burning bush of God's Word and decided that I would do what He called me to do rather than go on with my life the way I had planned. (I still have to make that decision every day.) That

> **To say yes to God is to receive a new status before God and a new direction in life.**

call was the reason I can say, *your response to God's call is the single, most transforming event in your life—all else flows from it.* Nothing has been the same since I said yes to God's call. To say yes to God is to receive a new status before God and a new direction in life. Everything is at risk when you say yes to God. This truth is why so many people cannot and do not answer God's call for their lives. Only those who say yes can know the excitement of seeing God work through them.

✚ **You may have had a similar experience when you thought that if you said yes to God, nothing would ever be the same. Record that experience below. Include your response to God. You may still be dealing with how to answer God. That's OK. Your Identity Group will pray for you at the next meeting.** _____
_____
_____
_____
_____
_____

God's Call on Paul's Life

If you grew up attending church, you will recognize this story. If you recently said yes to God's call to follow Jesus, this may be new to you. In either case, God's call to Saul of Tarsus is a model of how your life can change if you accept God's call. Turn to *Acts 9:1-31* in your Bible.

Lessons from a Former Bully

What can you learn from this historical event? What can you apply from Paul's experience on the road to Damascus? What lessons can you learn from a former church bully? Let me offer some insights.

1. *When God calls, pay attention and do what He says! (Acts 9:3-7).* God knocked Saul down and blinded him with the light of His presence. God showed Moses a burning bush. You may not experience God's presence in that way. A member of our church recalls a friend who prayed to trust Christ and immediately became sober after an 18-hour binge. He knew God had saved him and empowered him to overcome alcoholism. God may not do something that dramatic in your life, but He is always making His call known to you.

Saul was stunned. He asked, *"Who is that?"* Jesus answered with short, clear instructions. Saul was strong-willed, headstrong, and task-oriented. Jesus dealt with Saul dramatically to get his attention. When Jesus got his attention, Saul obeyed.

✚ **Write about an encounter you have had with God. It may not be dramatic, but just as real. Did you do what you sensed or heard God telling you to do?** _____
_____
_____
_____

2. *Accept the apparent limitations God may put on your life in order to redirect your priorities toward Him (Acts 9:8-9).* When Saul opened his eyes, he couldn't see. The light of Jesus had blinded him. He was led into the city where he lay for three days. God completely disabled this strong man in order to begin a process of redirecting his priorities. God's goal was to accomplish His purposes, not make Saul comfortable. God blinded Saul so that he could see things God's way.

Sometimes God puts limitations on your life in order to redirect your priorities toward His call. He may not knock you down and blind you, but don't overlook setbacks in your self-made plans as possible opportunities for God to change how you see things. That time of inconvenience may be the very time God uses to allow you to refocus your life.

✛ **Briefly write about a time when God used a sickness or a setback to refocus your life goals. What did you learn about God?** _____

_____

_____

_____

_____

_____

3. *Listen to those God may send to clarify His purposes in your life (Acts 9:10-16).* God would not speak directly to Saul after the encounter on the road. This was another way God brought this powerful man into submission to His call. Saul was used to dealing with the "head man." Being blind and hearing from a messenger rather than God was unusual for Saul. God, however, had changed Saul's will after three days of helplessness. Saul listened to Ananias as if he were listening to God. This reluctant witness gave God's message to Saul. Ananias' words became God's words to the one sent to tell all people about Jesus.

✛ **God may have used others to clarify His call on your life. Write in the margin the name of one of those people and record how that person helped you clarify God's will for your life.**

4. *Begin immediately to do what God has called you to do (Acts 9:18-25).* As in the rest of his life, Saul did not waste any time carrying out his orders. The difference now was that his orders came from God, not what he thought was right. He got up, was baptized, ate some food, and regained his strength. He was ready to go, and go he did. Rather than heading to the synagogue to stir up opposition to the Christians, he went where he had gone before to recruit people to follow Jesus! A lot of head scratching went on that day. Saul didn't stop and try to figure out what God wanted him to do and all the implications involved. Reflection on God's call would come later. Now it was time to be obedient.

✛ **Write a brief account of a time when you immediately did what God told you to do. It may have been as simple as walking across the street to pray with a neighbor. You may have picked up the phone and called the church to serve in a ministry.**

_____

_____

_____

_____

_____

God can use Saul's experience to teach you how to respond to Him when He calls you. That is one of the reasons it is recorded in Scripture. God's call on Saul's life and Saul's response to that call is an example of what can happen in your life if you hear God's call and say yes. Moses and Paul are biblical characters who were called to do something for God. Each man said yes to God, and both were never the same. Each man also experienced the power and presence of God as he lived his life under God's call rather than pursue his ideas about life.

SUMMARY

- Everything as you have known it can potentially change when God calls you to join Him on mission.
- God broke into Saul of Tarsus' life to call him to carry the good news of Jesus to all ethnic groups.
- When God calls, pay attention and do what He says!
- Accept the apparent limitations God may put on your life in order to redirect your priorities toward Him.
- Listen to those God may send to clarify His purposes in your life.
- Begin immediately to do what God has called you to do.

PERSONAL REFLECTION

✛ **Prayerfully complete these activities in your Identity Journal.**

1. **What decisions are you considering in your life now that can directly affect your relationship with God?**
2. **If you knew the story of God's call on Saul's life, what did you learn from today's lesson you had overlooked before? If this was the first time you read the story, what got your attention?**
3. **What lessons did you learn from Saul's experience with Jesus on the Damascus road that you can apply to your life today?**
4. **Has God called you to the same mission as Saul through Jesus' commandment to make disciples of all ethnic groups?**

DAY 4

ALL OF YOU!

The Lord had said to Abram, "Leave your country, your people and your father's household and go to the land I will show you" (Gen. 12:1).

TODAY YOU WILL ...

○ share personal feelings about what a call looks like in a person's life;
○ challenge the misconception that calling equals career;
○ review biblical characters God called who invested everything they had and were in the work of God; and,
○ take time to assess areas of your life in which God's call does not have an influence.

We have confused the biblical idea of *calling* with *career* in today's church. Let me demonstrate. Four people stand in front of you—a nurse, a public school teacher, a lawyer, and a pastor. Based on your experiences, which one would you most likely choose as the one who had answered God's call in his or her life?

If you chose the pastor, as I did, you would probably be in agreement with most Christians. We assume that someone who gave up a career in the marketplace to preach and lead people in the church surely had followed God's call, while the others pursued their own desires. Certainly a pastor is living his life in commitment to what God wants him to do. It's easy to think the nurse, teacher, and lawyer aren't quite as "called" as the preacher, or they, too, would be out preaching or on the mission field.

Many Christians tend to think that unless you have forsaken all to live in a foreign country "doing" missions or in a parsonage, you have not really accepted God's call for your life. We have mistaken call for career. God's call affects every aspect of our lives. When you say yes to God, it does not change who signs your paycheck. It changes what you do with who you are, what you make, and what you have.

When God called a person it had nothing to do with whether he was a warrior, shepherd, farmer, tax collector, or Pharisee. God's call was never about vocational counseling. It was always about joining Him in what He was doing to redeem His creation. I never find pastor or prophet in Scripture as categories for jobs at a job fair. Career is our designation for a job path. Career is not in the vocabulary of the Bible.

Calling, on the other hand, is in the Bible. Regardless of one's job, God called men and women to be instruments of His work on earth. God often used the skills the person had learned to enhance that call, but the call, not the career, was God's interest.

What is the true nature of *call?* One writer, Os Guinness, writes, "Calling is the truth that God calls us to himself so decisively that everything we are, everything we do, and everything we have is invested with a special devotion, dynamism, and direction lived out as a response to his summons and service."[1]

God's call is so decisive in a person's life that it affects every aspect of that life. All we are, all we do, and all we have are the God-given resources to do what God has called us to do. God's call is not about where we send our résumé, but about changing our direction and purpose in life—no matter where we work! Simply put, a Christian's life is a gracious response to God's call to follow.

⊕ **Write your definition of "call."** _____
_____
_____
_____
_____
_____

Testing an Idea

Let's test the premise that calling has little or nothing to do with choosing your career and everything to do with what you do with what you know, what you have, and who you are. We will take a quick survey of examples in the Bible to see if this premise holds up.

THE FATHER OF FAITH

⊕ **Read Genesis 12:1-3. What did God call Abram to do? What did He promise Abram?** _____
_____
_____
_____
_____

⊕ **Read Genesis 12:4-5. How did Abram respond to God's call?**
_____
_____
_____

> *Calling has little or nothing to do with choosing your career and everything to do with what you do with what you know, what you have, and who you are.*

God called Abram to leave his home and go to a promised land. God promised to make Abram the father of a great nation that would be a blessing to many. Abram obeyed God's call, packed up everything, and began the journey to a place he had never been before. This is why the New Testament writer to the Hebrews honored him as a man of faith when he wrote, *"By faith Abraham, when called to go to a place he would later receive as his inheritance, obeyed and went, even though he did not know where he was going" (Heb. 11:8)*.

God's call was so decisive that Abram did not ask any questions, but packed up all of his belongings and family and obeyed God.

A FARMER TURNED PROPHET

✚ **Read Amos 7:14-15. What was Amos doing when God called him to bring a message to the people of Israel?** _____

_____

_____

_____

_____

Amos is one of the prophets. He, however, was neither a prophet nor a prophet's son. Amos was a shepherd and cared for sycamore-fig trees. God called him to fulfill the role of a prophet for God. That call took him away from his daily tasks to proclaim God's message to the people. But he did not change "jobs" to become a prophet. The call of God was so decisive that he left everything and did what God told him to do.

God called both of these people and others throughout Scripture to join Him in His eternal work. This call changed everything in their lives. When God calls a person to join Him in His work, everything in his or her life is affected and everything becomes a resource to serve God's call.

God's Call on Your Life

We have agreed that God has called you to accept His gift of salvation and to make disciples of others. So, you can't say, "I haven't been called." Take a moment and reflect on this statement:

> As his disciple, I am not necessarily learning how to do special religious things, either as a part of "full-time service" or as a part of "part-time service." My discipleship to Jesus is, within clearly definable limits, not a matter of what I do, but how I do it. And it covers everything, "religious" or not.[2]

✚ **Write in the margin areas of your life you may have separated from God's call for you to follow Jesus. Be prepared to share them with your Identity Group.**

Areas of my life I have separated from God's call. _____

_____

_____

SUMMARY

- We often confuse the biblical idea of calling with career.
- In the Bible, when God called a person, it had nothing to do with whether he was a warrior, shepherd, farmer, tax collector, or Pharisee.
- "Calling is the truth that God calls us to himself so decisively that everything we are, everything we do, and everything we have is invested with a special devotion, dynamism, and direction lived out as a response to his summons and service."
- God calls every believer to join Him in His eternal work. This call changes everything in his or her life.
- Your discipleship to Jesus is, within clearly definable limits, not a matter of what you do, but how you do it. And it covers everything, "religious" or not.

PERSONAL REFLECTION

Prayerfully complete these activities in your Identity Journal.

1. **Do you tend to think that those in full-time Christian service have received more of a call from God than you? Why?**
2. **Explain the relationship between vocation and calling. How does Os Guinness' definition of calling help you understand the nature of God's call on a person's life?**
3. **With which biblical characters do you relate most closely? Abraham going to Canaan? Amos speaking for God? Why?**
4. **You may have identified several areas of your life in which God's call has not made an impact. Return to the list you made in the margin. Ask God to show you how He wants you to use those areas as ways to live out His call on your life.**

---

[1]Os Guinness, *The Call: Finding and Fulfilling the Central Purpose of Your Life,* (Nashville: Word Publishing, 1998). All rights reserved.
[2]Dallas Willard, *The Divine Conspiracy* (San Francisco: Harper Collins, 1998), 284.

DAY 5

A LIFE WORTHY OF YOUR CALL

"I urge you to live a life worthy of the calling you have received. ...
There is one body and one Spirit—
just as you were called to one hope when you were called" (Eph. 4:1,4).

TODAY YOU WILL ...

○ read a story that illustrates how you can become like Jesus;
○ review God's call in the lives of people you have studied this week; and,
○ list some examples of how you will live when you say yes to God's call.

Calvin Miller tells the following story.

I have told several times that wonderful story about a hunchback Persian prince, whose destiny it was to be king one day. He was so tragically deformed, however, that many in the kingdom could barely stand to think of the day when the deformed prince would assume the throne. Then the prince made an odd decree: He ordered the royal sculptor to carve his statue out of white marble, exactly as he would look if he had no deformity. When the statue was finished, he had it brought to the center of the palace.

Then, when the glorious statue was in place, the oddest kind of ritual began. Each day, this bent, deformed prince came to the tall stately statue of himself and took off his shirt. He then turned his own ugly spine toward the straight and regal back of his alter ego. He would back up to this statue and do all he could to throw his own shoulders against the stone shoulders of the statue, attempting to make his back as straight as that of the statue. Always he tried in vain.

Nothing deterred his spirit, however. Sun, wind, the days and indeed the very years could not stop his unusual routine. The years ground on, and his spirit of discipline never flagged. Then one day, his soul was brought alive, for he overheard some palace gossip say that they had noticed that the prince's odd physical litany appeared to be working: The prince did not appear to be so bent as he once had been. His zeal caught new flame. Then, who could measure the joy of that glorious day when he at last removed his shirt, backed up to his stone look-alike, and felt the naked thrill of cold marble on his own warm shoulders. Discipline and desire had at last made him like the image.[1]

Dr. Miller's story illustrates how a person can become like the image of his or her life as God desires it to be. This happens through daily discipline and desire. You are changed as you seek to be like the "stately statue" of Jesus in the center of your life. Great rejoicing comes as you draw closer to being like the person God has called you to become. Saying yes to God means conforming your life to what He has called you to become.

Trust and Obey

This week we have examined how God's call is the single, most transforming event on a person's life. We observed how Moses, Paul, and others said yes to God's call and how their lives were never the same after that.

✠ **Go back through this week's lessons and review the biblical characters who said yes to God. Write the name of the one you relate to best and why. Be prepared to share your answer in your Identity Group.** _____

_____

_____

_____

_____

Every positive response to God's call to salvation and to follow Him has a practical implication in how you live. Just as Peter left his nets and Abram left his homeland when they received God's call, so you will experience drastic changes in your life as you follow Jesus. This can only happen if you trust and obey God.

To obey is to do what Jesus says to do. Matthew obeyed Jesus when he got up from the tax table and followed Him. The rich young man disobeyed Jesus when He told him to sell everything and give it to the poor. You cannot become like Jesus until you follow Jesus. You cannot follow Jesus until you obey His call.

> *To obey is to do what Jesus says to do.*

> *You cannot follow Jesus until you obey His call.*

Your identity in Christ is based upon your trust in Jesus and your obedience to His call. You can experience the life-transforming presence of Christ only when you put your trust in Him and become willing to obey what He tells you to do. Jesus intended for us to be like Him. That's why He said, *"Follow me." Jesus meant for His disciples to follow Him and to do what He did. When Jesus washed the disciples' feet He said, " 'I have set you an example that you should do as I have done for you' " (John 13:15).* Jesus does not want you to ritualize what He did that night. He does want you to be willing to dress like a servant and act like a slave in order to serve others. If you have the heart of Jesus, you will be willing to act like Jesus.

Being transformed into the likeness of Jesus is not just part of the Gospels. The rest of the New Testament calls you to live a life that shows evidence that you are following Jesus.

Implications of the Call

Paul was in prison. God's promise that he would suffer for the name of Jesus had come true. While a prisoner for the Lord, he wrote to the Christians in Ephesus to explain who Jesus was in light of competing philosophies and religions. (See *Eph. 1–3.*) When he had completed his explanation of Jesus, he taught his readers how to live in light of their relationship with Jesus. Paul wanted them to know that their new spiritual relationship with Jesus Christ had practical implications.

⊕ **Read Ephesians 4:1. What did Paul urge his readers to do?** ____
_____
_____
_____
_____
_____
_____

Paul urged his readers to live a life worthy of the calling you have received. You can also translate the phrase, *walk in a manner worthy of the calling with which you have been called* (NASB). Walk is the biblical word for a person's lifestyle. Another interpretation may be, *let your lifestyle reflect that you have received God's call.*

Paul told Christians to live a certain way because they had been called into a relationship with God through Jesus Christ. Their relationship in Christ had implications in how to live. They were to live in such a way as to show others they had become worthy of a relationship with God. Paul's prominent word for their relationship with God was *called.*

⊕ **Read Ephesians 4:2-4. Describe the Christian way of life.** ___
_____
_____
_____
_____

> **If you have the heart of Jesus, you will be willing to act like Jesus.**

> **As a prisoner for the Lord, then, I urge you to live a life worthy of the calling you have received (Eph. 4:1).**

> **Be completely humble and gentle; be patient, bearing with one another in love. Make every effort to keep the unity of the Spirit through the bond of peace. There in one body and one Spirit—just as you were called to one hope when you were called (Eph. 4:2-4).**

✦ **What are some of the characteristics of a Christian who has received God's call to salvation?** _____

_____

_____

_____

_____

_____

_____

_____

> Be completely humble and gentle; be patient, bearing with one another in love. Make every effort to keep the unity of the Spirit through the bond of peace (Eph. 4:2-3).

> "Take my yoke upon you and learn from me, for I am gentle and humble in heart, and you will find rest for your souls" (Matt. 11:29).

> Therefore, since we have been justified through faith, we have peace with God through our Lord Jesus Christ (Rom. 5:1).

Paul spelled out what a life lived worthy of God's calling looks like. He wrote about it in *Ephesians 4:2-3*. He listed characteristics and actions of how those who said yes to God's call would live their lives. Every area of their lives would be affected by the presence of Christ. They were to be humble and gentle like Jesus. (See *Matt. 11:29*.) They were to be patient, which was one of the evidences of God's Spirit in their lives. (See *Eph. 4:2*.) They were to bear each other's cares with the love of Jesus. And, they were to maintain unity through the bond of peace brought to their lives through Christ *(Rom. 5:1)*. Living worthy of their calling meant going each day to the person of Jesus in the center of their lives and trying to straighten their sin-deformed backs against the perfect image of Jesus.

A Look Ahead

Just as Moses and Paul were never the same after saying yes to God's call, so your life cannot remain the same after you have received God's call. The following weeks of this study will spell out many of the implications of saying yes to God's call on your life. We will see how you actually become a new creation in Christ, how you gain a new status and standing with God, and how you will discover an entirely new way of life as you follow Jesus.

As you study these implications of your new identity in Christ, you will have to decide each day to continue to follow Him. Jesus told us to consider the cost of such a decision. He gave us this illustration:

> *"Suppose one of you wants to build a tower. Will he not first sit down and estimate the cost to see if he has enough money to complete it? For if he lays the foundation and is not able to finish it, everyone who sees it will ridicule him, saying, 'This fellow began to build and was not able to finish.' … In the same way, any of you who does not give up everything he has cannot be my disciple"* (Luke 14:28-30,33).

God has called you in Christ Jesus to follow Him and live your life in such a way to let others know you are His disciple. You must consider the cost of trusting and obeying Jesus and what it means to find your identity in Christ. It will cost you your life, but what you gain is far more valuable than what you will give up.

SUMMARY

- Saying yes to God means conforming your life to what He has called you to become.
- Trusting that God has called you means obeying God's word.
- Paul did not tell his readers to live in such a way in order to be worthy of a relationship with God. Paul told Christians to live a certain way because they had been called into a relationship with God.
- In your new identity in Christ, you have to decide each day to follow Him. Jesus told us to consider the cost of such a decision.

PERSONAL REFLECTION

⊕ **Prayerfully complete these activities in your Identity Journal.**

1. **What did Calvin Miller's story mean to you? How do you relate to the prince in the story?**
2. **Saying yes to God's call has serious implications on those who receive it. In today's lesson, you chose one person with whom you most related. With whom did you least relate? Why? What was it God asked that person to do that is so foreign to your life?**
3. **Paul wrote to the Ephesian Christians encouraging them to live worthy of their calling in Christ Jesus. Write in your own words what Ephesians 4:1 means to you.**
4. **Jesus warned that there is a great cost to following Him. Why is that so? Why do so many people not count the cost before following Jesus?**

---

[1]Calvin Miller, *Walking with Saints* (Nashville: Thomas Nelson, 1995), 219. Used by permission.

WEEK 3

MY SPIRITUAL DNA

This week you will ...
- examine the biblical reasons for why you need a new life in Christ (Day 1);
- review Jesus' teaching of a second birth and how that new birth allows you to have victory over your sinful nature (Day 2);
- examine the biblical teachings of your new life in Christ and consider its implications on how you live (Day 3);
- examine the biblical doctrine of creation and what it means to be a "new creation" in Christ (Day 4); and,
- answer the question, *Can you experience a second birth, receive a new life, and become a new creation and still live like you lived before those events?* (Day 5).

Memory Verse
Therefore, if anyone is in Christ, he is a new creation; the old has gone, the new has come! (2 Cor. 5:17).

Does anything really happen to you when you accept in faith that Jesus is the Son of God and you say yes to God's call? Yes! When you read the Bible people's lives are dramatically changed. People-pleasing fishermen become bold spokesmen for God. Demon-possessed lunatics walk peacefully back into their hometowns to live quietly for God. Ordinary people stand boldly before the powers that be and defy threats of torture and death to tell others about Jesus. Cowards become courageous. The weak become strong. The people of the Bible who encounter Christ become totally different people, not just devotees to a new way of thinking.

The reason Christianity is not a self-help course is because it is not about your changing yourself but about God transforming you. You and I are incapable of spiritual transformation in our natural-born bodies. Our nature must change before our lives can change.

The process begins with a new birth. The Holy Spirit of God begins to permeate every part of your life to transform you into the likeness of God's Son, Jesus. The Bible describes your spiritual transformation like the birth and growth of a child into adulthood. You are born again through faith, and you grow into a mature relationship with God as God's Holy Spirit changes you into the likeness of Jesus. You are a "new creation." You don't change yourself. God changes you from the inside out.

DAY 1
WHY I CAN'T CHANGE

I do not understand what I do. For what I want to do I do not do, but what I hate I do (Rom. 7:15).

TODAY YOU WILL ...

○ review Paul's explanation of how sin rules in your nature;
○ examine the biblical teachings about sin in your life;
○ answer questions about your struggles to do right and your
○ continual failures to do so; and,
○ examine what the Bible says about a new nature and how you can receive it.

Shawn (not his real name) "walked the aisle" and was baptized when he was nine. He went to church through high school, but he began to lose interest in church the closer he came to college. Shawn is pretty happy with his life—except he has never experienced the kind of spiritual change he learned about in Sunday School. His life is normal; he has no bad habits or criminal record. He goes to church occasionally but he doesn't understand what his pastor is talking about.

The stories of people in the Bible seem impossible to Shawn. He has concluded that people are in the Bible because they are out-of-the-ordinary. Shawn wonders why there is no one like him in Scripture. He stays away from church because he feels that everyone there must have figured it all out, and they are experiencing what he wants. Friends from school seem to have it all together at church. He knows better, though. He sees many of them on Friday nights with his other friends. Shawn wonders what is wrong. He just can't quite beat old habits and sinful acts in his life. Christianity frustrates more than helps with his life.

> *Who you are determines what you do.*

> We know that the law is spiritual; but I am unspiritual, sold as a slave to sin. I do not understand what I do. For what I want to do I do not do, but what I hate I do. And if I do what I do not want to do, I agree that the law is good. As it is, it is no longer I myself who do it, but it is sin living in me. I know that nothing good lives in me, that is, in my sinful nature. For I have the desire to do what is good, but I cannot carry it out. For what I do is not the good I want to do; no, the evil I do not want to do—this I keep on doing. Now if I do what I do not want to do, it is no longer I who do it, but it is sin living in me that does it (Rom. 7:14-20).

⊕ **Write a sentence or two describing what you have experienced or heard others say about faith and the Bible. Be prepared to share this in your Identity Group.**

_____

_____

The Need for a New Nature

If your identity is in Christ and the goal of the Christian life is to be transformed into the likeness of Christ, why do so few persons experience what God desires for their lives? Most people overlook the fact that a fundamental, spiritual change must take place in their lives to allow God to work. What must change? Your basic nature must change before God can work powerfully in your life. Who you are determines what you do. This is why the identity issue is so important for the Christian.

You are born with a nature that is opposed to the things of God. The Bible literally calls it your flesh. Paul wrote, *"I am of flesh, sold into bondage to sin" (Rom. 7:14,* NASB). Flesh was your natural state when you were born. Left unchecked and not transformed, your natural state leads you away from God and sells you into the bondage of sin. This natural, sinful nature is the source of your addictions, self-absorbing attentions, and actions that hurt others. It separates you from God, your Creator. Your sinful nature causes conflict between your desire to follow and be like Jesus and your need to follow and be like the world.

A Saint's Cry for Help

Like Shawn, you may wonder whether people in the Bible ever experienced the same challenges you do. And, if they did, how did they find help? Paul, the apostle, would be considered by most a saint. God changed his life and transformed him. He did great things for God. But did he ever experience what you and I experience in life? Let's see.

⊕ **Read Romans 7:14-20. What was Paul's problem? Describe it in your own words.** _____

_____

_____

_____

What was the source of Paul's problem? _____

_____

_____

How would you describe Paul's emotional state? Can you relate to his feelings? If so, how? _____

_____

_____

_____

_____

Paul wrote under the inspiration of the Holy Spirit to Christians in Rome to explain the answer to the question, How are sinful people accepted by Holy God? In *Romans 7* we find the height of his discussion about sin and its power in people's lives. The problem he described was that he could not do what he wanted to do, and he ended up doing what he hated to do *(v. 15)*. He even did the evil he did not want to do *(v. 19)*.

The source of his problem was his *sinful nature (v. 18)*. This was the core of who he was. *Sin living in me* caused him to do what he knew was wrong *(v. 17)*. How did he know what was wrong? The laws of God pointed out his shortcomings before Holy God *(vv. 15-16)*. This sin defined by God's laws controlled his decisions. It seemed that he wasn't the one making his decisions. Sin seemed to be calling all the shots. Paul sounded frustrated in this passage. He seemed completely at a loss of what to do with this state of life.

✦ **Read Romans 7:21-25. After his frustration with living the way he did, what was Paul's conclusion about why things were the way they were?** _____
_____
_____

What was his cry for help? _____
_____
_____

What was the answer to his cry? _____
_____
_____

Paul concluded that there were two laws at work in his life: the law of evil and the law of God *(v. 21)*. While in his mind he agreed with how God wanted him to live, in his daily decisions he was made prisoner to the law of evil *(vv. 22-23)*. It was literal warfare in his life to do what God wanted him to do and actually overcome sin's power to do it! He was a slave to God's law in his mind, but in his natural state he was a slave to the law of sin *(v. 25)*. Without help, he could only see his life as a continual battle between these two laws.

In frustration, he cried out, *"What a wretched man I am! Who will rescue me from this body of death?" (v. 24)*. The struggle with sin and the seeming impossibility to overcome it caused Paul (and anyone who has been honest with themselves) to see his wretched state and to cry out for deliverance. He admitted he could not overcome the influence of his sinful nature without help. Experience taught him that just agreeing with God would never fundamentally change him.

What was the answer to his cry? He shouted, *"Thanks be to God"* the answer to my problem is *"through Jesus Christ our Lord!" (v. 25)*. Paul couldn't help himself out of the cycle of sin. The solution to the sin problem in Paul's life was Jesus Christ.

> *So I find this law at work: When I want to do good, evil is right there with me. For in my inner being I delight in God's law; but I see another law at work in the members of my body, waging war against the law of my mind and making me a prisoner of the law of sin at work within my members. What a wretched man I am! Who will rescue me from this body of death? Thanks be to God—through Jesus Christ our Lord! So then, I myself in my mind am a slave to God's law, but in the sinful nature a slave to the law of sin (Rom. 7:21-25).*

Your Cry for Help

OK, you now know there is someone in the Bible who understands what you are going through. Paul can definitely identify with your struggle with sin and your desire to live for God. His story is your story. God inspired Paul to write what he did so you could understand more fully the things of God.

⊕ **Reflect on the following questions. You will not be asked to share your answers with your Identity Group.**

What struggles in your life allow you to understand what Paul talked about? _____
_____
_____

Can you accept the fact that unless you get help beyond your own efforts you will not be able to overcome the grip sin has on your life? ○ Yes ○ No ○ Not sure

Will you accept the reality that your natural state draws you away from God? ○ Yes ○ No ○ Not sure

Have you ever cried out in frustration like Paul over how you are living your life? ○ Yes ○ No **If yes, briefly describe your experience.** _____
_____
_____

Have you ever acknowledged that without Jesus Christ you are stuck in the cycle of sin? ○ Yes ○ No

Have you ever confessed that your only hope is through Jesus Christ our Lord? ○ Yes ○ No **Write your personal statement of confession.** _____
_____
_____

A New Nature

Paul explained how to live a life of victory over sin. He wrote how *"through Christ Jesus the law of the Spirit of life set me free from the law of sin and death" (Rom. 8:2).* Christ Jesus brings a new condition to your life that frees you from the influence of your natural state of sin. When Jesus Christ replaces your sinful nature with a new nature, the Bible says you will then be controlled by the Spirit, not your sinful self. (See *Rom. 8:5-7.*) You can have life and peace and know the joy of living the abundant life Jesus promised His followers *(John 10:10,* NASB). You can overcome evil and bad habits. You can live a life worthy of your calling with the new nature birthed in you through Christ Jesus.

How do you get this new nature? How does the Spirit of God become part of your life so you can know peace and victory in your life? The answers are in the remainder of this week's study.

SUMMARY

- A fundamental, spiritual change must take place in your life to allow God to work.
- You are born with a nature opposed to the things of God.
- Paul concluded that there were two laws at work in his life: the law of evil and the law of God *(Rom. 7:21-22)*. While in his mind he agreed with how God wanted him to live, in his daily decisions he was made prisoner to the law of evil *(vv. 22-23)*.
- You can have life and peace and know the joy of living the abundant life Jesus promised His followers *(John 10:10)*.

PERSONAL REFLECTION

⊕ **Prayerfully complete these activities in your Identity Journal.**

1. **If you have a "Shawn" in your life, take a moment to pray for this person. Ask God to show you ways to tell your friend of the victory God desires for their life.**
2. **In Romans, Paul described the power of sin in your life without the presence of God. How would you describe this to your friend you just prayed for?**
3. **Locate the section of today's session, "Your Cry for Help." Write a letter to God summarizing your thoughts. Honestly explain your feelings about the condition of your life.**
4. **Have you experienced the power of God over sin in your life? If so, write briefly about it. If not, name an area of life with which you struggle.**

DAY 2

A SECOND BIRTH

"I tell you the truth, no one can see the kingdom of God unless he is born again" (John 3:3).

TODAY YOU WILL ...

❍ be introduced to the concept of "spiritual DNA";

❍ examine Jesus' words to a religious leader about a second birth;

❍ review the biblical teachings about your behavior under the influence of sin; and,

❍ review what the Bible teaches about how you can live with the Spirit of God in control.

Receiving new "spiritual DNA," or, a spiritual code, is an analogy of what happens when you enter a relationship with God through Jesus Christ. God infuses the very code or pattern of God into your spirit. The presence of God's Holy Spirit begins to change you into the likeness of His Son after the pattern of His holiness. How this happens is not really a new analogy. Jesus called it being "born again."

In 1997, a team of scientists at the Roslin Institute, Edinburgh, UK, announced to the world that they had cloned a sheep. They named her Dolly. Cloning was not new, but the cloning of an adult mammal that grew into an identical replica is what caught the world's attention. Would humans be next? was the prevailing question. The team in England cloned a second sheep, and the experiments continue.[1]

Cloning is the extraction of the genetic code (DNA) from one living thing and its infusion into the growing form of another living thing. As the second being grows, it follows the identical code of the first and grows into the exact form of the first. Scientists use the technique in agriculture, medicine, and husbandry. The process can alter the development of a plant or animal. It can also create an identical twin.

You may be wondering, *Why the science lessons today?* Cloning, with all of its ethical problems, is a 21st century analogy of what happens in your life when you enter into a faith relationship with Jesus Christ. It can serve as an analogy of how you are fundamentally changed so that you can live in victory over sin and realize your identity in Christ.

A Second Birth?

Jesus spoke in word pictures to help people understand spiritual truths. One evening, a leading religious leader came to where Jesus was staying. In their conversation Jesus told the man, *"no one can see the kingdom of God unless he is born again" (John 3:3).* The guy asked the next question for all who hear the statement for the first time, *"How can a man be born when he is old? … Surely he cannot enter a second time into his mother's womb to be born!" (v. 4).*

⊕ **Read John 3:5-8. What did Jesus say to explain His previous statement?** _____

_____

_____

How did Jesus describe "everyone born of the Spirit?" _____

_____

_____

Jesus taught that each person must experience two births. One is of water or a natural birth initiated and produced by human parents. The second is of the Spirit or a spiritual birth brought about by the Spirit of God. Jesus said, *"Flesh gives birth to flesh, but the Spirit gives birth to spirit" (v. 6).* The physical can only give birth to the physical. Its genetic code or DNA can do nothing more. Jesus, on the other hand, described a second, separate birth from our natural one in order to see the kingdom of God. The Spirit of God gives birth only to spirit. Its genetic code is spiritual and produces spiritual beings.

This second birth is like cloning.[2] (Hang with me here. Remember that analogies are loose associations that communicate general references, not exact details.) In cloning, the living embryo is injected with the DNA of the original living being. The receptor being then develops after the coded patterns of the original. In the second birth Jesus speaks of, the living but sinful person is infused with the Spirit of God that begins to grow within the person's life. Its code is spiritual. Its pattern is godly. If it is nurtured through the process of discipleship, the receptor being can take on the characteristics of the Original.

Why is this second birth necessary? In day 1 we talked about how you are naturally drawn away from God by your natural state. Your sinful nature is this natural state in which you were born. It is the source of your inability to do anything right for God. Paul, however,

> *Jesus answered, "I tell you the truth, no one can enter the kingdom of God unless he is born of water and the Spirit. Flesh gives birth to flesh, but the Spirit gives birth to spirit. You should not be surprised at my saying, 'You must be born again.' The wind blows wherever it pleases. You hear its sound, but you cannot tell where it comes from or where it is going. So it is with everyone born of the Spirit" (John 3:5-8).*

talked about deliverance from that helpless state of sin through Jesus Christ. You can live beyond the natural code of sin in your life.

You can now see that Jesus provides an analogy of how you can live a victorious life over sin by experiencing a second birth, a birth that infuses an entirely different spiritual code in you. The first birth fills your life with a physical and natural code that corrupts your possibilities to experience the powerful presence of God. The second birth provides a spiritual DNA that places in your life God's Spirit that empowers you to live a new life for God. This pattern can transform who you are and, therefore, what you do.

Your Spiritual DNA

You are who you are physically because of your genetic makeup. You have a certain genetic code that began to guide your development at conception. While you are not carrying around a genetic identity card, you can observe some of the physical evidences of your genetic code.

✶ **Go back to week 1, day 1 and review the list of the "fingerprints" on your life. These are some of the physical characteristics by which you determine your identity. You have the fingerprints of your sinful nature in your life also. Let's take a look at some of those.**

✶ **Read Galatians 5:16-21. How does the Bible describe the relationship of your sinful nature and the Spirit?**
○ **They get along like rival siblings.**
○ **They live peacefully together in harmony.**
○ **They are similar but have some differences.**
○ **They are essentially different and in conflict with each other.**

Does your sinful nature allow you to do what you want to do?
○ **Yes**   ○ **No**

How does verse 17 reinforce Romans 7:14-20? _____
_____
_____
_____
_____

List observable characteristics of a person who lives in his natural state of sin (Gal. 5:19-21). _____
_____
_____
_____
_____

The Bible clearly teaches that your sinful nature is in conflict with the Spirit of God. The two are contrary in essence and in how they show themselves in your life. The result of living by your natural state is to be unable to do what you want to do. (See *Gal. 5:17.*) This truth reinforces

---

So I say, live by the Spirit, and you will not gratify the desires of the sinful nature. For the sinful nature desires what is contrary to the Spirit, and the Spirit what is contrary to the sinful nature. They are in conflict with each other, so that you do not do what you want. But if you are led by the Spirit, you are not under law. The acts of the sinful nature are obvious: sexual immorality, impurity and debauchery; idolatry and witchcraft; hatred, discord, jealousy, fits of rage, selfish ambition, dissensions, factions and envy; drunkenness, orgies, and the like. I warn you, as I did before, that those who live like this will not inherit the kingdom of God (Gal. 5:16-21).

Paul's confession that the reason he does what he hates is in his sinful nature. (See *Rom. 7:14-20*.) *Galatians 5:19-21* lists how sin manifests itself in behavior. If your spiritual code is sin, then your life will be filled with sinful things. The list of behaviors in *verses 19-21* is a representative list of what your sinful spiritual code will produce.

If our analogy of spiritual DNA holds up, that means you can observe some Christlike spiritual characteristics in your life. These would be present as the result of God infusing His Holy Spirit into your being at the time of your "second birth."

✦ **Read Galatians 5:22-24. What does the Bible call this list of characteristics?** _____
_____
_____

What are the characteristics of a life that God has filled with His Spirit? _____
_____
_____

How do these characteristics find their way into a person's life? ___
_____
_____

> *The fruit of the Spirit is love, joy, peace, patience, kindness, goodness, faithfulness, gentleness and self-control. Against such things there is no law. Those who belong to Christ Jesus have crucified the sinful nature with its passions and desires (Gal. 5:22-24).*

The Bible calls this list the *fruit of the Spirit*. Fruit is a biblical term for a person's behavior that results from who they are essentially. Jesus used the phrase as a way for His disciples to tell whether a person was a true or false prophet *(Matt. 7:15-20)*. Good trees produce good fruit. Bad trees produce bad fruit. In Galatians, the fruit of the Spirit is behavior or characteristics produced by the *good tree* of God's Spirit. These nine characteristics make up a representative list of what the presence of God's Spirit will produce.

If you're a little confused from today's study, maybe sharing my personal experience will help. I was born with a nature that is bent toward sin and away from the things of God. Left in that state I can neither have a relationship with God nor know the joy of living a godly life. I can't do what I want to do, and I end up doing the very things I hate. I'm helpless. Jesus said I enter His kingdom through a second birth. I don't understand that fully, but I trust Him. I confess my sinfulness and ask that His Spirit come and take control of my life. Through my second birth in Christ, I begin to experience the characteristics of love, joy, and peace. It's like something different is working in my mind and heart. When I read the Bible, I discover that that "something" is the Spirit of God that became part of my being at the second birth. It's like I received a new spiritual DNA whose code allows me to live like Jesus. The characteristics I experience are the "fruit" or evidence of the Spirit in my life. I begin to win a victory here and there over my old ways of living. I am filled with joy more each day.

SUMMARY

- Cloning is a 21st century analogy of what happens in your life when you enter into a faith relationship with Jesus Christ.
- Jesus taught that each person must experience two births: a natural birth initiated and produced by human parents and a spiritual birth brought about by the Spirit of God.
- The spiritual birth provides a spiritual DNA that places in your life the "code" of God's Spirit, empowering you to live a new life for God.
- If your spiritual code is sin, then your life will be filled with sinful things. The list of behaviors in *Galatians 5:19-21* is a representative list of what your sinful spiritual code will produce.
- In *Galatians 5:22-23* the nine characteristics of the fruit of the Spirit make up a representative list of what the presence of your spiritual DNA in Christ will produce.

PERSONAL REFLECTION

⊕ **Prayerfully complete these activities in your Identity Journal.**

1. **Have you experienced what Jesus called a second birth?**
   ○ **Yes** ○ **No If yes, when did that take place?**
2. **Write your personal testimony. Incorporate the concepts of a second birth and new spiritual DNA.**
3. **When you read about the conflict between your sinful nature and the Spirit, did it remind you of a conflict you have experienced in your life? Briefly describe one experience.**
4. **If someone asked you to list the "fruit" or evidence of the Spirit in your life, what would you list?**

---

[1]From *http://www.encyclopediabritannica/cloning of dolly*
[2]The Bible uses the technique of grafting branches onto another plant as an analogy for how non-Jewish people were assimilated into Christianity *(Rom. 11:17-21).*

DAY 3

A NEW LIFE

"For you died, and your life is now hidden with Christ in God. When Christ, who is your life, appears, then you also will appear with him in glory" (Col. 3:3-4).

TODAY YOU WILL ...

○ read the story of one person's new life that resulted from another's desire to share;
○ examine the biblical analogy of being raised with Christ;
○ list the earthly and heavenly things you pursue each day;
○ review the amount of time you spend thinking on things of this world; and,
○ examine the implications of your new life in Christ.

Stephanie needed a new liver. She would die without one. As she waited for a donor, her health deteriorated. Her husband and the church prayed for God to provide a healthy organ for her sick body. Knowing that to get an organ someone would have to die, the church prayed that the person be a Christian. Finally, one night their pager went off, and Stephanie was rushed to the hospital. The next day, Stephanie had a new liver. Since that day, Stephanie also has had a new life as her health steadily improves. One day, She met the husband of her organ donor. Her donor was a Christian woman who joyfully gave her organ so another could live. Stephanie volunteers at the hospital and encourages people to consider giving their organs so others can live. Stephanie has a new life because she has a new organ.

Another Picture
Stephanie's story is another analogy of what happens when you receive through faith a new life through God's Spirit, the Giver of Life. The presence of God's Spirit in your life results in characteristics you never

knew before your decision to trust and obey Him. Once you have been born into the family of God, your focus changes. You desire different things. You pursue different goals. You wonder why your previous life seemed so wonderful. You really had not seen anything compared to this life. You now have a story to tell. You have a new reason to get out of bed each day.

Read Colossians 3:1-2 and complete the statements below.

Since, then, you have been _____

Set your heart on _____

Set your mind on _____

> Since, then, you have been raised with Christ, set your hearts on things above, where Christ is seated at the right hand of God. Set your minds on things above, not on earthly things (Col. 3:1-2).

Paul, the writer of the letter to the Colossians, wrote that since you have been raised with Christ, certain things have happened in your life. Like being born again, being raised with Christ is a picture in language you can understand that describes the mysterious reality of how you come into a relationship with Christ. You are raised with Christ through faith to live a new life for Him *(Rom. 6:4).*

Being raised with Christ causes you to refocus your life. The Bible says to *"set your hearts on things above" (Col. 3:1).* You can also translate that phrase *pursue the things above.* Rather than seeking the things of this world, a new relationship with Christ refocuses your life on things beyond this world—godly things. Your relationship with Christ changes your target.

Be prepared to share your answers to these questions with your Identity Group.

What are some "earthly things" you pursue? _____
_____
_____
_____
_____
_____

What are some "things above" you pursue? _____
_____
_____
_____
_____
_____

If you were to take your day organizer or calendar and count the time spent on earthly things and things above, which of the two would get the most time? (Check one.)
○ **earthly things**   ○ **things above**

Paul also called his readers to, *"Set your minds on things above, not on earthly things"* (Col. 3:2). Literally, the phrase is *think on things above, not on things on the earth.* Being raised to a new life in Christ refocuses your attention. We will see later in this study that a major part of your transformation into the likeness of Christ is a transformed mind. (See *Rom. 12:1-2.*) A new relationship with Christ draws your thinking away from the way this world thinks toward the things of God. Paul spoke of this when he wrote to the Philippians. (See *Phil. 4:8.*)

⊕ **Make a list of "earthly things" most people think about.**

_____
_____
_____
_____

Make a list of "things above" God would have you think about.

_____
_____
_____
_____

What do you think about most? (Check one.)
○ **earthly things**   ○ **things above**

A new life in Christ ushers in a new focus in life. Both your heart and mind are drawn toward the things of God and away from the things of this earth. You find yourself pursuing godly living rather than seeking self-gratifying activities. You spend more time reading the Bible than magazines for help in how to live each day. You watch less television and spend more time with other Christians. Since you have been raised with Christ, you are a new person.

Christ, Who Is Your Life

Just as Stephanie's donor had to die in order to give her life, Jesus died to give you new life in Him. Jesus' death purchased your new life. This death/life analogy is another picture of how you find your identity in Christ. According to the Bible, before you were raised with Christ, you died with Him, too. In Colossians, Paul used the same association when he wrote, *"you died, and your life is now hidden with Christ in God"* (Col. 3:3).

To be raised with Christ means you have died with Christ. When I baptize a person, I quote *Romans 6:4.* As I place the person under the water, I say, *"We were therefore buried with him through baptism into death."* As I bring them out of the water, I say, *"just as Christ was raised from the dead through the glory of the Father, we too may live a new life."* Baptism is a visible testimony of what happens in your life when you put your trust in Jesus. It is a picture of the death of your old spiritual self (sinful nature) to the birth of your new life in Christ. Your old self no longer lives, but Christ lives in you.

> *Finally, brothers, whatever is true, whatever is noble, whatever is right, whatever is pure, whatever is lovely, whatever is admirable—if anything is excellent or praiseworthy—think about such things (Phil. 4:8).*

✚ **Write about your baptism experience. Remember the emotions, sights, and sounds. Recall who baptized you and who witnessed your baptism. Record what that experience meant to you and how you have lived your life since that event. Be prepared to share this with your Identity Group.**

_____
_____
_____
_____
_____
_____
_____
_____

Your relationship with Christ through His death and resurrection has eternal consequences, too. The next verse in today's passage says, *"When Christ, who is your life, appears, then you also will appear with him in glory" (Col. 3:4).* This verse reinforces that Christ is your life—the focus of your pursuits and thoughts. It also teaches that because of your relationship with Him you will *"appear with him in glory."* Earlier in this letter, Paul reminded his readers that *"Christ in you, [is] the hope of glory" (Col. 1:27).* According to the Bible, if Christ is in you through a faith relationship—a new birth, new spiritual DNA, a transplant of His Spirit—then you will stand with Him forever.

Implications of Your New Life

Who you are determines how you live. What implications does your new life in Christ have for you now? Let's answer that question from the next verses in Paul's letter to the Colossians.

✚ **Read Colossians 3:5-11. The Bible tells you to put to death and rid yourselves of certain things in your life. List them.**

_____
_____
_____
_____

In verses 9 and 10, Paul uses another phrase of how we make the things of God part of our lives. Write the phrase here.

_____
_____

What is Paul's conclusion (v. 11)?

_____
_____
_____

Put to death, therefore, whatever belongs to your earthly nature: sexual immorality, impurity, lust, evil desires and greed, which is idolatry. Because of these, the wrath of God is coming. You used to walk in these ways, in the life you once lived. But now you must rid yourselves of all such things as these: anger, rage, malice, slander, and filthy language from your lips. Do not lie to each other, since you have taken off your old self with its practices and have put on the new self, which is being renewed in knowledge in the image of its Creator. Here there is no Greek or Jew, circumcised or uncircumcised, barbarian, Scythian, slave or free, but Christ is all, and is in all (Col. 3:9-11).

Your new life has implications for how you live. In *Colossians 3:5-11,* Paul expresses in his letter some of what you do when God creates a new life in you. Each behavior in the list is the result of living in your sinful nature. In verses 9 and 10, Paul introduces the idea of taking off old clothing and putting on new. You "take off" the old self with its influences, and you "put on" your new self when you come into a faith relationship with Jesus. You clothe yourself in your new self *"which is being renewed in knowledge in the image of its Creator" (Col. 3:10).* You experience spiritual transformation as your new self in Christ is renewed through the presence of Christ.

⊕ **Read Colossians 3:12-17. List some of the implications of living clothed in your "new self."**

_____
_____
_____
_____
_____

Your behavior is different when you clothe yourself in the things of God. The fact is summarized in *verse 17.* Read it again. *Whatever you do,* means your whole life, which is all you say and do. Your whole life changes when you receive a new life in Christ. When you accept God's call, you will never be the same. God intends for you to live differently when you receive a new life through His presence.

SUMMARY

- Stephanie's story is an analogy of what happens when you receive through faith God's forgiveness and His Spirit.
- Your relationship with Christ changes your goal.
- Your relationship with Christ changes your thinking.
- Baptism is a visible testimony of what happens in your life when you put your trust in Jesus.
- You experience spiritual transformation as your new self in Christ is renewed through the presence of Christ.

PERSONAL REFLECTION

⊕ **Prayerfully complete these activities in your Identity Journal.**
1. **What can you apply from Stephanie's story to your life? Are you in need of a new life? Are you waiting for someone to help you? Do you know someone in a similar situation? What are you doing to help them?**
2. **Reflect on what the biblical idea of being raised with Christ means. You may want to read the Gospel account of Jesus' resurrection or a depiction of heaven from Revelation.**

Therefore, as God's chosen people, holy and dearly loved, clothe yourselves with compassion, kindness, humility, gentleness and patience Bear with each other and forgive whatever grievances you may have against one another. Forgive as the Lord forgave you. And over all these virtues put on love, which binds them all together in perfect unity. Let the peace of Christ rule in your hearts, since as members of one body you were called to peace. And be thankful. Let the word of Christ dwell in you richly as you teach and admonish one another with all wisdom, and as you sing psalms, hymns and spiritual songs with gratitude in your hearts to God. And whatever you do, whether in word or deed, do it all in the name of the Lord Jesus, giving thanks to God the Father through him (Col. 3:12-17).

3. Make a list of what you can do to set your heart on things above (Col. 3:1). Make a similar list of ways you can set your mind on things above (Col. 3:2).

4. Review Colossians 3:5-11. Write behaviors in that list that are still part of your life. Ask God to transform your life by removing those behaviors. Read again Colossians 3:12-17, and write those things you have done recently. Pray that your "new self" in Christ will have a greater influence on you today as you clothe yourself in the things of God.

DAY 4

A NEW CREATION

Therefore, if anyone is in Christ, he is a new creation; the old has gone, the new has come! (2 Cor. 5:17).

TODAY YOU WILL ...

○ examine the biblical doctrine of a fallen creation and its transformation through the work of Christ;
○ write a personal statement of belief based on what the Bible teaches about creation;
○ examine what it means to be a new creature in Christ; and,
○ examine the immediate implications of being a new creation.

The first words of the Old Testament are, *In the beginning God created the heavens and the earth (Gen. 1:1).* The first words of the Gospel of John in the New Testament are, *In the beginning was the Word, and the Word was with God, and the Word was God (John 1:1).* This is not a coincidence. One purpose of the Bible is to tell of a new creation that redeems the old one. The pivotal event of the new creation was the coming of Jesus. Jesus Christ, the Word, is the new beginning for all of creation. He is also Creator of all creation. (See *John 1:3; Col. 1:16-17.*)

The fallen creation, all living things including people, is in decay and disorder because of sin. Sin is rebellion by people against the purposes of God. (See *Gen. 3*.) Creation is doomed to destruction without intervention from its Creator. The New Testament tells how the Old Testament state of affairs will be transformed to be in line with the purposes of God again.

✤ **Read Romans 8:19-21. Place a check by the words used in those verses to describe creation as it is now.**
○ **waiting in eager expectation**
○ **frustrated**
○ **evolving toward completeness**
○ **enslaved to decay**
○ **just as God created it**

The Bible teaches that creation waits eagerly for the revelation of the sons of God *(v. 19)*. Why? Creation has been subjected to frustration (*"futility," v. 20*, NASB) and enslaved to decay because of the sin of people. (See *Gen. 3:17-19*.) Creation lives in hope that God will free it from these things and bring it *into the glorious freedom of the children of God (Rom. 8:21)*.

✤ **Read Romans 8:22-25. Place a check by the words to describe creation and people in it.**
○ **happy and content**
○ **groaning as in the pains of childbirth**
○ **content with our condition**
○ **waiting eagerly for adoption as children of God**
○ **filled with despair**
○ **hope in God's redemption through Jesus Christ**

The Bible teaches that all of creation groans as if it were in childbirth *(Rom. 8:22)*. I've never had a baby, but I know that as I stood by my wife when our children were ready to be born, groaning was part of the deal! People who have a relationship with Jesus Christ experience the same "groaning" or discontent while waiting eagerly for their ultimate adoption as children of God *(v. 23)*. This "adoption," which we will study in depth later, includes the *redemption of our bodies*. The transformation of our earthly bodies is confirmed in the biblical teaching about our resurrected bodies. (See *1 Cor. 15:35-58*.) The Bible teaches that the Christian lives in the truth that God's purpose will be completed in creation *(Rom. 8:24-25)*.

✤ **Write in the margin a personal "doctrine of creation" completing the phrase, I believe ... Use the biblical information you have just studied as the basis of your statement. Be prepared to share this with your Identity Group.**

I believe ...

_____
_____
_____
_____
_____
_____
_____
_____

Your personal statement of belief on creation will help you see another reason you need a relationship with God through Christ. As a being created by God, you suffer the same decay and chaos as the rest of creation unless the Creator, Jesus Christ, intervenes.

A New Creature

You may be wondering: *What does an understanding of the state of creation have to do with me and my identity in Christ?* Since you are part of the created order, it has everything to do with you and me. Adam's and Eve's sin in the garden of Eden is the reason you and I and all creation need a Redeemer. The consequence of their sin is the source of our sinful nature, and that prevents us from having a relationship with God. We need to become part of a new created order to experience the fullness of God in our lives.

The Bible teaches that Jesus Christ, the Creator, is the *beginning and firstborn from among the dead (Col. 1:18)*. Jesus' resurrection from the dead began a new order of creation. God forgave the sin of the first order and destroyed death, the *last enemy (1 Cor. 15:26)* of those born under that order, when Jesus died, was buried, and raised on the third day. Those who are in Christ are part of that new order. These two orders coexist until God judges the first order and brings into reality a new heaven and new earth. (See *Rev. 21:1*.)

🔵 **Read 2 Corinthians 5:17. List the three things Paul teaches are real in a person who is in Christ.**

1. _____
2. _____
3. _____

> *Therefore, if anyone is in Christ, he is a new creation; the old has gone, the new has come! (2 Cor. 5:17).*

Paul teaches: (1) You are *a new creation;* (2) *the old has gone;* and (3) *the new has come!* First, the Bible says you are a new creation. The word *creation* can also be translated *creature* (NASB). The second translation makes the message more personal. It means that you become a new creature when you put your trust in Jesus Christ! You become part of the new order of creation established at Jesus' resurrection.

Paul also wrote that when you become a new creature, *the old has gone.* We use the phrase *passed away* sometimes to refer to those who have died. Another popular translation of this phrase is, *"the old things passed away" (2 Cor. 5:17, NASB)*. The old things died. They no longer have an influence in your life. This truth is consistent with the idea of "taking off the old self."

The new has come is the third consequence of your relationship with Christ. The word for *new* in the original language is the same as the one for *new* in a *new creation.* It commonly means *brand new.* It is not cleaned up like a used car is polished for sale to another owner. It is brand new. First time on the showroom floor. Fresh from the factory. In your relationship with Christ, it means an entirely new way of life. Old ways of living are gone. Old influences of sin no longer control you. You have a new start like a newborn baby.

✛ **Describe some of the "old" that has left your life since you have come into or have grown in your relationship with Jesus.**

_____

_____

_____

_____

Describe some of the "new" ways of living that are part of your life since Jesus came into your heart. Be prepared to share your answers with your Identity Group.

_____

_____

_____

_____

A New Reason to Live

The Bible says a new relationship with God means a new purpose for living. Who you are determines how you live. If you are a new creature in Christ, then how you live your life will be new also. We will go deeper into the implications of our identity in Christ later, but I would like to illustrate this truth while we are in this passage.

> *Who you are determines how you live.*

✛ **Read 2 Corinthians 5:18-20. What is the recurring word in these verses?** _____

_____

_____

What did God give those He reconciled to Himself? _____

_____

_____

What has God committed to those He reconciled? _____

_____

_____

What is the new role of those God reconciled to Himself? _____

_____

_____

_____

The primary concept in these verses is reconciliation. This is an important word in the New Testament. Reconciliation describes how God makes your broken relationship with Him whole again. You were an enemy of God in your sin, but God reconciled you (made you right before Him) through the death of His Son. (See *Rom. 5:10-11.*) Reconciliation makes you just before Holy God. You cannot make this happen by your efforts. God has done it all in Jesus Christ. This is the implication in *2 Corinthians 5:18, All this is from God.* You are a new creature through the reconciliation you have received in Christ Jesus.

Now that you have been reconciled to God, God has given you the *ministry of reconciliation (2 Cor. 5:18)*. The word for *ministry* can also mean service. Your new identity gives you a new reason to live, a service to perform. Part of God's call on your life through salvation is to share with others the message of reconciliation. What is the content of that ministry? *That God was reconciling the world to himself in Christ, not counting men's sins against them (2 Cor. 5:19).*

Your identity in Christ is *Christ's ambassador (2 Cor. 5:20)*. The word that is translated *ambassador* is actually a verb form in its original language. The phrase can be translated, we act as *ambassadors on Christ's behalf.* The implication is that you serve as God's representative when you offer His message of reconciliation to others. Who you are has changed what you do.

SUMMARY

- The fallen creation, all living things including people, is in decay and disorder because of sin. Sin is rebellion by people against the purposes of God *(Gen. 3)*.
- The Christian lives in the truth that God's purpose will be completed in creation *(Rom. 8:24-25)*.
- Jesus Christ, the Creator, is the *new beginning* and *firstborn from among the dead (Col. 1:18)*.
- The Bible teaches: (1) You are *a new creation;* (2) *the old has gone;* and (3) *the new has come! (2 Cor. 5:17)*.
- As a new creature, God has identified you as His ambassador who carries the message of reconciliation to all people *(2 Cor. 5:19-20)*.

PERSONAL REFLECTION

⊕ **Prayerfully complete these activities in your Identity Journal.**

1. **Some people believe that we are created good and that, somewhere along the way, we turn bad. Based on the biblical doctrine of creation, what is your response to that belief?**
2. **What are some ways you physically, emotionally, and spiritually "groan" while waiting for the completion of God's redeeming work in your life?**
3. **How would you describe what it means to be a "new creature" to someone who knows nothing about the Bible?**
4. **Write a job description for an "ambassador for Christ."**
5. **List the names of two or three people with whom you need to share the message of reconciliation.**

DAY 5

NEW LIFE MEANS NEW CONTAINERS

" 'No one pours new wine into old wineskins. If he does, the new wine will burst the skins, the wine will run out and the wineskins will be ruined. No, new wine must be poured into new wineskins' "
(Luke 5:37-38).

TODAY YOU WILL ...

○ answer the question, Can you experience a second birth and live the way you always have?;
○ apply the principles of Jesus' story about new wine and old wineskins to your new life in Christ; and,
○ propose ways you can allow your "new self" desires to find a place of greater influence than your "old self" habits.

✦ **Can you experience a second birth, receive a new life, become a new creation, and still live like you did before those events?**
○ **Yes** ○ **No** ○ **Not sure**

✦ **Jesus told a story that helps answer that question. Read Luke 5:36-38. What point was Jesus making?**

_____

_____

In Jesus' day cloth obviously was not preshrunk before it was sewn for clothing. Jesus used a common sense analogy from His culture when He said that you don't sew a new piece of cloth to repair an old, shrunk piece of clothing. If you did and then the new cloth shrunk, you would destroy what you were trying to repair. The same is true with pouring new wine into old wineskins. New, unfermented wine gives off gases as it ages. A stretched leather wineskin would eventually explode with new wine, because it could expand no more. When the new expanded in the old you would lose both the wine and its container. Everyone in Jesus' day understood the parts of the analogy. But did they get His point?

Jesus told this story to explain that His coming inaugurated a new way of doing things. Jesus was saying, *Change because the rule of God has come.* Jesus taught that the new covenant He brought would not fit into the old covenant ways of doing things. Patches from the kingdom of heaven stitched on old covenant habits would tear apart both. New movements of God demand fresh containers to hold it.

This principle applies to every area of your life. It is especially true for your new relationship with God through Jesus. As we have seen from the Bible, you have been born into a new life through faith. This new life is like the new cloth and new wine in Jesus' story.

⊕ If you tried to integrate this new life into your old habits or lifestyle, what would be a logical conclusion? _____

_____

_____

_____

_____

_____

_____

_____

_____

The logical conclusion is that if you tried to patch your old habits with the new cloth of your new life, one would cause the other to tear. Let me give you a simple, non-threatening example.

You enjoy going to the movies every Saturday night. You look forward to sitting in the dark, eating popcorn, and seeing the latest special effects or romance story. You even go to two shows a night if they are films you want to see. It is no problem if you get in late at night. You love movies. You are a "late night" person, and mornings on the weekend don't start until about noon. When you were younger, your parents expected you to go to church on Sunday mornings. This practice has slipped and is optional for you to have a good weekend. If you have to make a choice, movies would win 90 percent of the time.

Then you have a life-changing experience with Christ. You encounter the resurrected Lord, and through faith you are born into a new relationship with God. You sense things are different. You long to know more about God and the Bible. You want to worship and praise God for what He has done in your life. But you still love movies.

✦ **It's Saturday night, and you are ready to go see the latest movie. The only ticket you can get is for the 10:00 p.m. showing. You want to say you were the first of your friends to see it, but you want to be fresh for worship on Sunday morning. What do you do? Check your answer below. Be prepared to share in your Identity Group.**

○ Go to the movie and plan to go to worship next week.

○ Go to the movie and hope you wake up in time the next morning for worship.

○ Pray before you go to church that the graphic images from the movie will not affect your thinking during worship.

○ Pass on the movie and arrive for worship refreshed and anticipating an encounter with God.

Most of us would try to fit both into our lives. And most of the time it seems to fit. But over a long period of time, if we apply Jesus' words, one of those choices would win out over the other.

✦ **According to Jesus' story, you cannot fit new life into old habits. Something related to your entertainment and worship habits would have to change. List two examples of what might have to change.**

1. _____

2. _____

The Rest of the Story

Jesus' story is consistent with what we have learned about the implications of having a new life in Christ. One reason you seldom see changes in your habits and priorities after a faith encounter with Jesus is because you neglect the truth that your faith in Jesus means following Him—following His example in every area of your life. The call of God on your life is to become like Jesus. If you choose to accept God's call, you must make choices about how you live. To try and keep the "old self" ways in "new self" clothing creates a conflict in your life.

✦ **Complete the chart below. In one column, list "old self" habits that are part of your life and dominate your lifestyle. Be honest. You can choose whether to share these answers with your Identity Group. In the other column, list "new self" desires God has put in your life.**

My "Old Self" Habits	My "New Self" Desire
_____	_____
_____	_____
_____	_____
_____	_____
_____	_____
_____	_____

✜ **Circle the one or two most significant habits and desires that, if you decided to pursue both, would cause conflict in your life. Choose one of those areas and write three things you could do today to allow your desires to overcome your habits.**

1. _____

_____

2. _____

_____

3. _____

_____

Jesus taught that a new life in Him destroys old ways of living. New wine demands new wineskins. New cloth is never used to patch old clothes. A new life in Christ demands new life choices. Patches of new spiritual clothing cannot be sewn on an "old self" life and be expected to fix the problem. New cloth only fits with new clothes.

SUMMARY

- You cannot experience a second birth, receive a new life, become a new creation, and still live like you did before those events.
- Jesus called for new ways of living because a new way of life had come in Him. Jesus taught that the new covenant He brought would not fit into the old covenant ways of doing things.
- If you try to patch your old habits with the cloth of your new life, one will cause the other to tear.
- One reason you seldom see changes in your habits and priorities after a faith encounter with Jesus is because you neglect the truth that your faith in Jesus means adopting His example in every area of your life.
- A new life in Christ demands new life choices.

PERSONAL REFLECTION

✜ **Prayerfully complete these activities in your Identity Journal.**

1. **You may have observed someone trying to pour "new wine" into "old wineskins." Describe that experience and the consequences of the efforts.**
2. **Reflect on ways your new life in Christ has caused conflict with the lifestyle you experienced prior to putting your faith in Jesus. Ask God to show you ways to resolve those conflicts by allowing your new life desires to overcome old habits.**
3. **Call a member of your Identity Group and offer to pray for him or her. Write down anything you could pray with them about before the next meeting. Do what you offer to do.**

WEEK 4
MY STATUS BEFORE GOD

This week you will examine ...
- your status before God without a relationship with Jesus Christ (Day 1);
- the biblical concept of justification, one way your status changes before God (Day 2);
- the biblical concept of redemption and review Jesus' work of salvation through His death on the cross (Day 3);
- how God has delivered you from the domination of evil in your life (Day 4); and,
- the biblical concept of sanctification and review biblical passages that describe holiness in past, present, and future tenses (Day 5).

Memory Verse
Therefore, since we have been justified through faith, we have peace with God through our Lord Jesus Christ (Rom. 5:1).

You probably had never heard of Diana Frances Spencer until she married Prince Charles of Wales. She came from common beginnings and only dreamed of being a princess. In July 1981, when she became the Princess of Wales, her status changed. She was no longer a distant relative of the royal family, she was now a member of the family. Not only did her identity change, her status changed. Through that marriage, Princess Diana enjoyed all the privileges of being heir to the throne of England. She would no longer be Diana Spencer. She would go down in history as Princess Diana. Even after her divorce from Prince Charles and her untimely death in a car accident, she is still remembered as Princess Di.

The change of status from unknown to royalty does not happen to many people. Even those who win a huge lottery or make millions never know the difference a genuine change in status brings. God can bring the greatest change in status to a person's life. Other people and their perception of you do not determine this status. It is measured by God's work in Jesus Christ.

In this week's study, you will discover how a relationship with Christ changes not only your identity but also your status before God. More important than becoming a prince or princess, you become a child of God! More important than other people declaring a new status in your life, God declares your ultimate status change: from enemy of God to child of God.

We will review how God works in our lives to change our status. We will rediscover ideas such as justification, redemption, deliverance, and sanctification. Each of these biblical concepts explains part of the process of how God changes our status and identity in Christ Jesus. We will seek to apply each important idea to our relationship with God through Jesus Christ.

DAY 1

YOUR CURRENT STATUS

"For if, when we were God's enemies, we were reconciled to him through the death of his Son, how much more, having been reconciled, shall we be saved through his life!" (Rom. 5:10).

TODAY YOU WILL ...

○ review how status is determined in your culture;
○ examine what your status is before God without a relationship with Jesus Christ;
○ discover how God saw you before you put your trust in Jesus; and,
○ review the biblical terms for how to experience the mercy of God instead of the wrath of God.

On the very first day of this study you identified different ways you define who you are. You completed the statement "I tend to evaluate who I am based on ..." You probably shared your responses with your Identity Group. That same list of indicators can apply to how others determine your status in life.

✦ **Return to your list in week 1, and review your answers (p. 9). Begin with those items and make a list in the margin on this page of things people use to determine the status of others. Examples may be wealth, membership on a team, class rank, or however your community defines status.**

An Audience of One

In our culture, status is determined by how others see you and place value on who you are. But, there is a more important someone who determines your ultimate status. That someone is God. No matter how your peers decide your place in community or history, your place before God is most important. You will not stand before your peers when you die to give account of your life. People's opinions of you will not matter when you are before Eternal God to explain why He should let you into His heaven. All that matters is your status before God.

You live before audiences. Your teachers may be your audience. Your boy or girlfriend or parents may be whom you are trying to please. God may be one of those you live your life in front of to gain recognition or status. Os Guinness, author of *The Call,* describes the audiences of your life: "Most of us, whether we are aware of it or not, do things with an eye to the approval of one audience or another. The question is not *whether* we have an audience but *which* audience we have.

"This observation underscores another vital feature of the truth of calling: *A life lived listening to the decisive call of God is a life lived before one audience that trumps all others—the Audience of One.*"[1]

Your nature is to live for the approval of others. But, a follower of Jesus seeks only the approval of his Lord and Savior. This is living before the "audience of one." This makes all the difference in how you live.

The Bible offers this advice about who should be your audience: *Whatever you do, work at it with all your heart, as working for the Lord, not for men, since you know that you will receive an inheritance from the Lord as a reward. It is the Lord Christ you are serving (Col. 3:23-24).* In all you do your audience should be the Lord.

To understand your true status, you need to have this Audience of One. If you seek the approval of others and ignore God's approval, you may end up with Nobel Prize status on earth but separated from God for eternity. Who is your audience?

✦ **List the names of those people in your life who are an audience for your actions. Be prepared to share your answers with your Identity Group.**

_____

_____

_____

_____

_____

What would change if God were my only audience? Write your answer in the margin.

God Is Holy and Expects the Same from You

Since God is truly the One who determines your eternal status, you should know something about Him and His nature.

> Just as he who called you is holy, so be holy in all you do (1 Pet. 1:15).

> Exalt the Lord our God and worship at his holy mountain, for the Lord our God is holy (Ps. 99:9).

> They were calling to one another: "Holy, holy, holy is the Lord Almighty; the whole earth is full of his glory" (Isa. 6:3).

> The wrath of God is being revealed from heaven against all the godlessness and wickedness of men who suppress the truth by their wickedness (Rom. 1:18).

> If, when we were God's enemies, we were reconciled to him through the death of his Son, how much more, having been reconciled, shall we be saved through his life! (Rom. 5:10).

✺ **Read the following passages of Scripture and write what they have to say about God's character.**
1 Peter 1:15 _____
Psalm 99:9 _____
Isaiah 6:3 _____

Circle the one repeating word in each of the verses that describes the character of God.

God is holy. This means God is separate and complete from His creation. To be holy is to be "wholly other" and perfect in every way. God is beyond our comprehension and cannot be approached because of His perfection and righteousness. But, what does God insist for you? God insists that you be holy as He is holy. (See *1 Pet. 1:15*.) But, you are not holy in your natural state. You learned this last week when you looked at your inability to change without the help of God. You also cannot have an acceptable status before God without His help. Let's see why.

Your Status Before Holy God

The goal of this study is to help you be transformed into the likeness of Christ. One area of transformation is your status before God in Christ. You cannot become like Jesus until you are in relationship with Jesus. You cannot be a member of the family of God until you are adopted into the family. Before we examine the biblical ideas about the process that accomplishes those things in your life, we need to determine how God sees you. We need to answer two questions: *What are God's eternal criteria for status in the family of God? and If God is Holy and I am not holy, what does that mean?*

✺ **Read the following passages. Write beside each one what it says about a person's status before God when he or she is without a relationship with Jesus.**

Romans 1:18 _____
Romans 5:10 _____
Galatians 3:10 _____
Ephesians 2:1-3 _____

The Bible speaks about the *wrath of God which is against all the godlessness and wickedness of men who suppress the truth by their wickedness (Rom. 1:18).* God's wrath is the opposite of His mercy. Wrath is God's holy response to sin and godlessness. You may say, "I'm not godless and wicked. What does God's wrath have to do with me?" *Galatians 3:10* states, *"Cursed is everyone who does not continue to do everything written in the Book of the Law."* If you cannot do everything God desires of you, then the Bible states you are cursed and deserve the wrath of God. Your status before God deserves His response of wrath. *Ephesians 2:3* states that in our sinful state we are *objects of wrath*. God's holiness demands He exhibit His wrath to those who do not live up to His holy standards.

The Bible also states you are an enemy of God before you are reconciled to God *(Rom. 5:10)*. An enemy of God! Can you think of a more powerful adversary? Can you imagine the possibilities if God chose to destroy His enemies? The Bible also states you are *dead in your transgressions and sins (Eph. 2:1)* without Christ. It would follow that if you were an object of God's wrath you would be dead! The biblical message is that you are dead from an eternal perspective, not just an earthly one. Your sins make death your status before God.

⊕ **What can you conclude about your status before the One who ultimately determines your eternal place?**

_____

_____

_____

You have the status of being an enemy of God and being dead from God's perspective when you are without a relationship with Christ. The most important audience who establishes your status is God, and from His holy perspective, you have no status at all.

Your New Status

This information was not designed to discourage you. But you need to know the truth behind your spiritual status before God. Only when you accept this truth will you be ready to know how your status can change before God. How that happens is what the rest of this week's study is about. The concepts of *justification, redemption,* and *sanctification* tell how God changes your status from enemy of God to knowing peace with God. You participate in the process, but, ultimately, it is the work of God in Christ Jesus that changes you.

⊕ **As a pretest to the rest of the week's study, write your description of the following concepts.**

Justification _____
Redemption _____
Deliverance _____
Sanctification _____

> *All who rely on observing the law are under a curse, for it is written: "Cursed is everyone who does not continue to do everything written in the Book of the Law"* (Gal. 3:10).

> *As for you, you were dead in your transgressions and sins, in which you used to live when you followed the ways of this world and of the ruler of the kingdom of the air, the spirit who is now at work in those who are disobedient. All of us also lived among them at one time, gratifying the cravings of our sinful nature and following its desires and thoughts. Like the rest, we were by nature objects of wrath* (Eph. 2:1-3).

SUMMARY

- "The question is not whether we have an audience but which audience we have."
- If God is truly the One who determines your eternal status, you should know something about Him and His nature.
- God is holy. This means God is separate and complete from His creation. To be holy is to be "wholly other" and perfect in every way.
- Your sins make death your status before Holy God.

PERSONAL REFLECTION

⊕ **Prayerfully complete these activities in your Identity Journal.**

1. Have you ever desired a different status than you now have? If so, describe it to an Identity Group member. If not, write reasons you are satisfied with your current status in life.

2. On page 79 you listed audiences in your life. Reflect on why those audiences have such a powerful influence. Write a prayer to God for understanding of their influence and for ways to seek only God's approval in all you do.

3. What would your daily life look like in light of Colossians 3:23-24? How would it change the way you live each day?

4. To hear that you are an enemy of God and that you are dead in sin are not pleasant thoughts. What were your first impressions when you read this description? If you have grown up in church, when did you first understand your natural status before God? How did you respond?

5. If you were to stand before God in eternity today, what would your status be?

---

[1]Os Guinness, *The Call: Finding and Fulfilling the Central Purpose of Life,* (Nashville: Word Publishing, 1998). All rights reserved.

DAY 2

MADE RIGHT BEFORE GOD

"Since we have been justified through faith, we have peace with God through our Lord Jesus Christ" (Rom. 5:1).

TODAY YOU WILL ...

○ examine justification, one way your status changes before God;
○ examine how the Bible teaches you are justified before God;
○ evaluate some misconceptions about justification; and,
○ write your definition of this important biblical concept.

Imagine standing before a judge in a courtroom. The judge is about to sentence you for a crime you committed and for which you have been found guilty. The judge has a reputation for being very strict and hard on criminals. You stand and wait to hear your sentence.

⊕ **If the judge were to sentence you in a manner similar to that of the biblical concept of justification, what would it be? Put a check by the statement that most reflects your understanding. Be prepared to share with your Identity Group the reason you chose your answer.**
○ **"Sir, you have been found guilty. I must sentence you to the maximum limits of the law so you will learn your lesson."**
○ **"Sir, you have been found guilty. That fact remains, but I have thrown out your sentence because I believe you are a good person who made a dumb mistake. You are free to go."**
○ **"Sir, you have been found guilty, but I am overturning that conviction. Your record will be cleaned up, and you will serve no jail time or pay any penalties. Have a nice day."**

○ "Sir, you have been found guilty of a serious crime. I must uphold that conviction. You deserve the maximum penalty of the law, death by lethal injection. I, however, have grown to love you and want you to live. The debt must be paid, however. My son, who also loves you and your family deeply, has agreed to pay your penalty with his life. You can go if you like. Your sentence is paid in full."

A Change of Status

Day 1 taught that God has declared you guilty, and you are the object of His wrath. One day you will stand before Jesus Christ as Judge. (See *1 Pet. 4:5*.) He will declare you righteous or guilty before Holy God. Without a change in status, you will suffer the consequences of your sin. How can your status before God change? That's the question of the week. It has a four-part answer. Today's study will examine the first part.

The biblical concept of justification answers the question, *How are sinful people made right before Holy God? Or, How can my status as enemy of God, object of God's wrath, and dead in sin change to a child of God, object of His mercy, and alive in Christ?* God demands that everyone possess a righteousness defined by His standards. Those standards are unachievable by anything you can do. You must become "right" in God's sight to have a right relationship with your Creator. Justification explains how this restored relationship happens.

The root concept in the verb *to justify* is "to put right with, to cause to be in a right relationship with."[1] In the New Testament this process of being put right with God is always God's loving action toward people. God changes your status before Him. You cannot affect that change on your own. How does the Bible explain this change?

⊕ **Read the following Scriptures and write how each describes what happens in the process of justification.**
Romans 5:1-2 _____
_____
Romans 5:16-19 _____
_____

Romans 5:1-2 describes a result of God's making us right before Him. Since your trust in Jesus' death and resurrection has made you right before God (justified), you now have peace with God. You are no longer someone who deserves God's wrath. Through trust in Jesus Christ, God has changed your status from a person at war with God to a person who is at peace with God. Peace is not a change in your feelings toward God, but a change in God's relationship with you. How does that happen? You gain access to this new status by trusting Jesus as Lord and Savior *(v. 2)*.

In *Romans 5:16-19* Paul describes how God's free gift of justification in Christ is different from the consequences of sin brought on by Adam. Sin brought judgment and condemnation *(v. 16)*. *The gift* was God's work through Jesus to make you right before Him *(v. 16)*. The result of Jesus' *act of righteousness* on behalf of all people brought life for all who will put their trust in Him *(v. 18)*.

> *Therefore, since we have been justified through faith, we have peace with God through our Lord Jesus Christ, through whom we have gained access by faith into this grace in which we now stand. And we rejoice in the hope of the glory of the Lord (Rom. 5:1-2).*

> *Justification is God's work through Jesus that makes you right before God so you can have a relationship with Him.*

Being Right Before God

Did you notice that through your brief search of the verses that nowhere does it say your actions make you right before God? In every instance it is the work of God through Jesus that makes your relationship right before God. Your participation in this process is to trust that God's work in Jesus is adequate. Justification is God's work. Your response of trust is all that is required of you.

The only way you can gain a new status before God is to receive it. Trusting God's work through Jesus to make you right before Him is the only way this change takes place. You trust God's word when He says trusting is the only way. This is part of your identity in Christ, too. You are who God says you are, not what you have earned on your own. Your identity before you trust Christ, remember, is enemy of God. Your identity after you trust Christ is a person at peace with God, made right before Holy God. Justification helps explain who you are in Christ.

✦ **Based on your study of justification, return to the activity on page 83. Write the reason why each of the judge's sentences is either correct or incorrect.**

1._____

_____

2._____

_____

3._____

_____

4._____

Here are my answers. The first response is not correct because being justified before God does not mean suffering the consequences of breaking the law. The second response is incorrect because while the conviction stands, the penalty remains to be paid. In justification, a payment still had to be paid for you to stand right before God.

The third response is invalid because God does not simply remove the conviction and sentence and wish you a happy life. The process is more serious than that. The concept of justification implies a guilty conviction with a penalty waiting to be paid. God does not remove either until His requirements for rightness are satisfied.

As strange as it may seem, the fourth response is the correct one. You are guilty, and the judge doesn't change the conviction. You deserve the death penalty, but for some reason the judge loves you and desires you to live. (A fact you did not know until the judge told you.) So, the judge and his son decide the son will die in your place so you can live. You have a choice to accept that payment or serve the sentence yourself. If you choose to accept the judge's offer, you walk away a found-guilty person who will live rather than suffer the maximum penalty of the law. You will live as if you have never been found guilty or sentenced, because the judge's son will die in your place.

> *Again, the gift of God is not like the result of the one man's sin. The judgment followed one since and brought condemnation, but the gift followed many trespasses and brought justification. For if, by the trespass of the one man, death reigned through that one man, how much more will those who receive God's abundant provision of grace and of the gift of righteousness reign in life through the one man, Jesus Christ. Consequently, just as the result of one trespass was condemnation for all men, so also the result of one act of righteousness was justification that brings life for all men. For just as through the disobedience of the one man the many were made sinners, so also through the obedience of the one man the many will be made righteous (Rom. 5:16-19).*

⊕ **How would you live your life differently if this happened to you? Respond below.**

_____

_____

_____

Without Christ you need a change of status before God. God knows this and has provided the sacrifice of His Son as an agent of change. If you will trust God, you can experience a change in status from enemy of God to a person at peace with God.

⊕ **To conclude this session, write your definition of justification below. Be prepared to share it with your Identity Group.**

_____

_____

SUMMARY

- One day you will stand before Jesus Christ as judge *(1 Pet. 4:5)*. He will declare you righteous or guilty before Holy God. Without a change in status, you will suffer the consequences of your sin.
- The root concept in the verb *to justify* is "to put right with, to cause to be in a right relationship with."
- Justification is God's work through Jesus that makes you right before Him so you can have a relationship with Him.
- Justification is God's work. Your response of trust is all that is required.
- Your identity after trusting Christ is a person at peace with God, made right before Holy God.

PERSONAL REFLECTION

⊕ **Prayerfully complete these activities in your Identity Journal.**

1. **How would an experience before a judge feel to you? Describe your emotions based on the answer you chose.**
2. **Since being justified by God means a change in status, write a paragraph to God, thanking Him for changing your status from being His enemy to giving you peace.**
3. **Have you ever been an "earn it" person, allowing what you had accomplished to define both your identity and your status before God? Write about how you lived your life. Or, explain how you are a "receive it" person.**
4. **Using your personal description of justification, compose an imaginary conversation with someone who has not trusted Jesus.**

---

[1]Johannes P. Louw and Eugene A. Nida, eds, *Greek-English Lexicon of the New Testament Based on Semantic Domains,* Vol. 1, (New York: United Bible Societies, 1988), 452, 34.46.

DAY 3

RESCUED BY GOD

In him we have redemption through his blood, the forgiveness of sins, in accordance with the riches of God's grace that he lavished on us with all wisdom and understanding (Eph. 1:7-8).

TODAY YOU WILL ...

○ read about a hostage crisis and write about how you would feel in a similar situation;
○ examine the biblical concept of redemption; and,
○ read the crucifixion story of Jesus.

I was in my office when the call came. I was on call with our local police department that week, and the dispatcher asked me to join the other chaplains at an elementary school on the other side of town. As I drove to the school, I listened to radio reports that told of a hostage situation developing in a day-care center. From those reports and police radio traffic, I learned a man had gone into the center and was keeping over 70 children and staff from leaving. He had a gun.

Most of the evening I sat with parents whose children were still in the center. We waited in the elementary school close to where the hostages were being held. I talked with the families about their children and how they longed for their safety. They wished the man no harm. They just wanted their children home. The gunman allowed different numbers of children to leave throughout the night. My eyes filled with tears as I watched families reunited after hours of fear and worry. I thought about how I would feel if those were my daughters in the day-care center. Finally, after 30 hours, the man gave up. SWAT team members rushed in and released the remaining children. The crisis was over. No one had been hurt, but many people were disturbed by the events.

✛ **Write some emotions you might experience if you were held in a hostage situation. Be prepared to share your feelings with your Identity Group.**

_____

_____

I don't know whether you have ever been involved in a hostage situation firsthand. That was my first (and I hope my last). The emotion I felt most was empathy with the parents who wanted their children back in their arms. Nothing is more painful than knowing someone the parents neither know nor trust is holding their child against his or her will, and there is nothing to do but wait. Those parents needed someone other than themselves to rescue their children.

Redemption Is Your Way to Freedom

In a real sense, you are held hostage by sin. You have seen how the Bible describes your status before God. Left in the bondage of sin, your eternal future is hopeless. How can your status before God change? Yesterday we examined justification as a way our status changes from being an enemy of God to having peace with God. Today we will examine redemption.

Let's review some biblical passages that describe redemption.

✛ **Read Ephesians 1:7. What two things do you receive by being in relationship with Christ Jesus?**

1. _____
2. _____

Read 1 Corinthians 1:30. What three things has Christ Jesus become for our benefit?

1. _____
2. _____
3. _____

> *In him we have redemption through his blood, the forgiveness of sins, in accordance with the riches of God's grace (Eph. 1:7).*

> *It is because of him that you are in Christ Jesus, who has become for us wisdom from God—that is, our righteousness, holiness and redemption (1 Cor. 1:30).*

The Bible states that being "in him"[1] means you have: *redemption through his blood,* and *the forgiveness of sins.* Both of these realities are part of God's grace shown to everyone who trusts Him *(Eph. 1:7).* Redemption comes from an ancient word that means "to release or set free."[2] Like the children in the day-care center, you are set free by the work of another. Unlike the day-care hostage crisis, a price was paid for your release. *Through his blood* is a way of saying that Jesus' death on the cross was the payment for your freedom.

The writer of the letter to the Hebrews wrote to Jewish people to explain why Jesus was the Messiah. He covered many topics, but an important one was the death of Jesus. *If Jesus was the Messiah, why did He die on the cross?* was a strategic question for all Jews. To answer that question, he wrote, *"In fact, the law requires that nearly everything be cleansed with blood, and without the shedding of blood there is no forgiveness"* (Heb. 9:22). God chose the shedding of a blood sacrifice as the way to atone for the sins of the people. (See *Lev. 16* for the annual Day of Atonement, or *Yom Kippur.*) Jesus' death, the shedding of His blood, was the final sacrifice required by God for people to have a right relationship with Him.

Paul explained to the Corinthian Christians that God chose the foolish things of the world to embarrass the wise. He chose a suffering Messiah to shame those who were powerful and who put weight in the things of the world *(1 Cor. 1:27).* God allowed Christians to be "in Christ," who is wisdom from God. And, in that relationship the one who trusts in Christ receives righteousness, holiness, and redemption *(1 Cor. 1:30).* Righteousness is the result of justification. Holiness is the result of sanctification. Redemption is the result of God's forgiveness of sins.

Remembering His Death

You were rescued from sin by Jesus' death on the cross. As foreign as it may seem to you, Jesus' shed blood is what purchased your freedom.

⊕ **Find a quiet place and read the account of Jesus' betrayal, unjust trial, and death on the cross. Each Gospel writer observed the events from a slightly different point of view. From the references below, choose the account you have not read or have not read recently, and read it in one sitting.**

Matthew 26:47–27:66   **Mark 14:43–15:47**
Luke 22:66–23:56   **John 19**

Jesus' death on the cross is how God satisfied His own requirements for righteousness. God completed His work to provide salvation for all who would trust Him through the historical events that took place in Jerusalem. What you have read is the ultimate act of love God has shown you. Jesus died on the cross in your place so you could have life.

SUMMARY

- In a real sense, you are held hostage by sin.
- The Bible states that being *in him* means you have *redemption through his blood,* and *the forgiveness of sins.*
- Jesus' physical death on the cross was an historical event that was part of God's plan to bring salvation to all who believe *(Col. 1:21-22).*
- The one who trusts in Christ receives righteousness, holiness, and redemption *(1 Cor. 1:30).*
- Jesus' death on the cross is how God satisfied His own requirements for righteousness.

PERSONAL REFLECTION

⊕ **Prayerfully complete these activities in your Identity Journal.**

1. **If you found yourself in a hostage situation, who would you want to rescue you? Would you try to create ways on your own to get out? Would you think first to help others get out or make sure your way out was secure before you helped others?**

2. **To redeem means "to rescue" or "free." What are some habits, thought patterns, or behaviors from which you desire to be rescued?**

3. **After reading what Jesus' death has done for you, how do you feel about who you are as a person God sees as forgiven, rescued, righteous, and holy? Write a couple of sentences describing how you feel about your identity at this stage of the study.**

4. **Describe your feelings about Jesus' death on the cross. Write a letter or poem or paint a picture to express your emotions for God's love and your appreciation to Him for sending His Son to die for you.**

---

[1]See the discussion of the meaning of "in him" in week 1, day 4.
[2]Johannes P. Louw and Eugene A. Nida, eds., *Greek-English Lexicon of the New Testament Based on Semantic Domains*, Vol. 1, (New York: National Book Printers, 1988) 488, 37.128.

DAY 4

DELIVERED FROM EVIL

"He has rescued us from the dominion of darkness and brought us into the kingdom of the Son he loves" (Col. 1:13).

TODAY YOU WILL ...

○ assess your beliefs about evil and Satan;
○ review biblical teachings about the source of temptation in your life;
○ examine God's promise that you can defeat evil and temptation; and,
○ examine how God has delivered you from the domination of evil.

✦ **Check below what you believe about evil, Satan, and demons.**
○ **Evil is the less human part of a person that causes him to do things not accepted by society.**
○ **The spiritual realm is real; Satan and demons dwell there.**
○ **Satan and demons can interact with the physical realm.**
○ **Angels are dead people who come back to earth to help others get to heaven.**
○ **Satan is a personification of all that is bad in people.**
○ **Demons are the way ancient people described psychological problems we now diagnose and treat through medicine.**
○ **Satan is a fallen angel who is hell-bent on the destruction of God's creation and His creatures.**
○ **Satan has a sphere of influence that the Bible calls a dominion.**
○ **Authorities, kingdoms, governments, and powers can be instruments of either good or evil.**
○ **You belong to the kingdom of darkness or the kingdom of light.**

The above statements are representative beliefs that people hold about evil and Satan. We live in a culture where evil is glamorized in popular films. Witchcraft is accepted as part of television story lines. Vampire slayers are heroes to many students. As a Christian, you cannot simply write off the reality of evil in the world. You also cannot allow the existence of evil to frighten you from living a victorious life in Christ. Until you find yourself in heaven, you will deal with evil and its influences daily. But, you do not have to be defeated by it.

Evil is a reality. While some may use it as an excuse not to trust God, its presence in the world affirms the Bible's description of reality. Evil is not external to you and me. To understand the extent of evil's influence in your life, you must realize evil is part of who you are in your sinful state. Its presence prevents you from becoming who God desires you to be. Even after God has made you right with Him, you can be tempted away from the things of God. Temptation is one way the Evil One seeks to prevent you from becoming like Jesus.

The Sources of Temptation

Temptation is whatever seduces you from a full and meaningful relationship with God. Temptation can come in any form and can lure you away with anything. Temptation is both external and internal.

Jesus' temptation at the beginning of His public ministry was a form of external temptation. Satan came to Jesus and sought to seduce Him away from doing God's will. (See *Matt. 4:1-11*.) Satan, the Accuser, came to Jesus in the wilderness. He offered Jesus three shortcuts to the kingdom. After this exchange in the desert, Satan left Jesus in the care of angels. Temptation can come from the direct influence of Satan.

The Bible also teaches that the world can be a source of external temptation. Your love for things of this world can draw your attention away from God. *First John 2:15-17* states the world lures you away from God through the desires of your natural drives ("the lust of the flesh"), your desire for what you see ("the lust of the eyes"), and your desire to accumulate things and achieve status ("the pride of life"). Your love for these things seduces you from living "in Christ."

You may have experienced external temptation. Satan himself may not have shown up, but a person or opportunity may have tempted you to turn your back on God's goal for your life. Things or people you may have seen or desired can be sources of temptation.

✦ **List some ways that temptation has come from an external source. Be prepared to share your answers with your Identity Group.**

_____
_____
_____
_____

Being sinful in nature, you naturally are drawn away from the things of God. This is why you need God's intervention in your life to claim a new identity. Temptation is part of your sinful, non-transformed self.

✦ **Read James 1:13-16. What is the source of temptation in your life?**

_____

> *When tempted, no one should say, "God is tempting me." For God cannot be tempted by evil, nor does he tempt anyone; but each one is tempted when, by his own evil desire, he is dragged away and enticed. Then, after desire has conceived, it gives birth to sin; and sin, when it is full-grown, gives birth to death. Don't be deceived, my dear brothers (Jas. 1:13-16).*

What is the progression of temptation to death?

_____

_____

The Bible teaches that temptation also comes from within. It is an internal reality. God is not the source of temptation. Your own evil desires seduce you away from doing what God desires for you. These desires give birth to actions, and those sinful actions result in death *(v. 15)*. Dallas Willard put it this way, "But when one receives and harbors [obsessive desires], one is 'pregnant with evil, gives birth to sin and the consequence is death or separation from God.' "[1]

⊕ **In the margin make a short list of natural desires in your life that have or could potentially lead to sinful actions. These are some of the internal sources of temptation in your life.**

Not Too Much to Handle

Jesus overcame external temptation from Satan by staying true to God's call on His life. You, too, can resist both internal and external temptation. God promises that you will always be able to resist temptation and remain in complete relationship with Him.

> *"But remember that the temptations that come into your life are no different from what others experience. And God is faithful. He will keep the temptation from becoming so strong that you can't stand up against it. When you are tempted, he will show you a way out so that you will not give in to it" (1 Cor. 10:13, NLT).*

⊕ **Underline the phrase in the verses above and on the previous page that gives you the most hope to resist temptation.**

You may be encouraged to know that your temptations are no different than what others are experiencing. You may find hope in the fact that God will never let you be tempted beyond what you can handle. Or, you may be surprised to discover that God provides a way out of every temptation so you will not sin.

God is involved in every aspect of your life. God has ultimate power over evil and its influence. You do not have to resign yourself to a life of sin if you have allowed God to transform you. God promises that you will never be tempted in any way other than anyone else has been tempted. God promises you can stand up against any temptation, internal or external, with His help. And, God promises He will show you a way out of every situation if you will look for it.

The greatest promise God gives us is that our Savior, our Deliverer, has been tempted in every way you and I have been tempted. The difference is that He never sinned! Christ is the One who stands up for us in the presence of Holy God and pleads our case.

⊕ **Read Hebrews 4:14-16. Why can you trust Jesus to understand your situation in the middle of temptation?**

_____

_____

List of natural desires:

_____

_____

_____

_____

_____

_____

_____

_____

Therefore, since we have a great high priest who has gone through the heavens, Jesus the Son of God, let us hold firmly to the faith we profess. For we do not have a high priest who is unable to sympathize with our weaknesses, but we have one who has been tempted in every way, just as we are—yet was without sin. Let us then approach the throne of grace with confidence, so that we may receive mercy and find grace to help us in our time of need (Heb. 4:14-16).

> *Dear children, do not let anyone lead you astray. He who does what is right is righteous, just as he is righteous. He who does what is sinful is of the devil, because the devil has been sinning from the beginning. The reason the Son of God appeared was to destroy the devil's work. No one who is born of God will continue to sin, because God's seed remains in him; he cannot go on sinning, because he has been born of God. This is how we know who the children of God are and who the children of the devil are: Anyone who does not do what is right is not a child of God; nor is anyone who does not love his brother (1 John 3:7-10).*

God's Work of Deliverance

Deliverance is a biblical word. Deliverance has been used in some circles to describe deliverance from evil spirits and to be synonymous with exorcism. While the word can have those meanings, the more common use of the concept in the Bible is to rescue persons from the darkness of evil and bring them into the kingdom of light.

You can overcome temptation because you have been delivered from the influence of evil. You can live a life that God transforms into the likeness of Jesus because you no longer live in the domain of evil but in the kingdom of light.

The Bible explains how you can tell someone who lives under the influence of evil from someone who does not.

🌐 **Read 1 John 3:7-10. Why do people do what is right?** _____
_____

If someone keeps on in the habits of sin, what does that say about him or her? _____

What did Jesus come to do? _____
_____

If you have been born again, what power does evil have on your life?
_____

How do you tell the difference between someone who is a child of God and someone who is a child of Satan? _____
_____

The Bible states that people do right things because they are righteous through a relationship with Christ. If a person continues to habitually sin, he remains under the influence of the Evil One, who has been sinning since the beginning of the world. Those who have been born into a relationship with God can overcome sin because God's Spirit lives within them. Your new relationship with God gives you the power to overcome internal and external temptations. You are able to defeat the influence of sin in your life. The difference between those who are children of evil and those who are children of God is that children of God obey God's commands and love others. *Who you are determines how you live your life.*

Evil and Satan are real. They are the enemies of God and barriers to experiencing a new identity in Christ. But you do not have to live in defeat to their influences. In Christ, you have been delivered from the dominion of evil and now belong to the kingdom of light. Christ delivered you. Now, live like you are free.

SUMMARY

- Evil is part of who you are in your sinful state. Evil prevents you from becoming who God desires you to be.
- Temptation is whatever seduces you away from a full and meaningful relationship with God.
- Temptation can come from the direct influence of Satan.
- Temptation is part of your sinful, non-transformed self.
- You do not have to resign yourself to a life of sin if you have allowed God to transform you.
- Your new relationship with God gives you the power to overcome internal and external temptations. You are able to defeat the influence of sin in your life.

PERSONAL REFLECTION

✚ **Prayerfully complete these activities in your Identity Journal.**

1. **You may have encountered evil directly. Write about your experience. Include your feelings and what you would do differently if it happened again.**
2. **You have learned about external and internal sources of temptation in your life. What did you believe prior to today's study about the source of temptation?**
3. **Respond to the following statement: "I can overcome every temptation in my life if I will just follow Jesus closely and do what He says."**
4. **Look at your lists of external and internal temptations in your life. Pray through each of those influences, thanking God they are not unique to you and that they are not more than you can handle with His help. Write a prayer asking Him to show you ways to escape the actions that would follow if you gave into the temptations.**

---

[1]Dallas Willard, *The Divine Conspiracy* (San Francisco: HarperCollins Publishers, 1998), 344.

DAY 5

MADE HOLY

"By that will, we have been made holy through the sacrifice of the body of Jesus Christ once for all" (Heb. 10:10).

TODAY YOU WILL ...

○ examine the biblical concept of sanctification;
○ review biblical passages that describe becoming holy in past, present, and future tenses; and,
○ examine Jesus' prayer that all of His followers become holy.

This week's study began with a review of God's holiness. You learned about God's work of changing your status through the person of Jesus Christ. You examined the concepts of justification, redemption, and deliverance—descriptions of how God has changed your status from enemy to having peace with Him. Today, you will examine a fourth concept of how God changes your status before Him. That concept is *sanctification*.

⊕ **Write a brief description of sanctification. Be prepared to share your answer with your Identity Group.**

_____
_____
_____
_____

You Have Been Made Holy

The root word for sanctification is *holy*. Sanctification is used in Scripture to describe the character of God and those people and things set apart for His service. It is also the root word for the New Testament title *saints,* which is used to describe Christians. You can translate *saints* as *holy ones* when referring to Christians. (See *Rom. 1:7; 1 Cor. 1:2*.) Christians are *holy ones* set apart by God for His service.

God requires holiness of those who are found in His presence. Sanctification is the process by which you are made holy; that is, acceptable by Holy God. God loves you. Jesus is proof of that love, but God's character does not allow Him to accept into His presence anything or anyone who is not pure and right according to His standards. Sanctification is God's work in your life to make you right before Him and to empower you to live a life set apart for His purposes.

You must examine the past, present, and future tenses to fully understand how God makes you holy. Paul referred to the Christians in Corinth as *"those sanctified in Christ Jesus and called to be holy" (1 Cor. 1:2)*; or, *"you who have been called by God to be his own holy people. He made you holy by means of Christ Jesus"* (NLT). Both translations express the past tense of God's action that makes the Christian holy. That action is Jesus' death on the cross. Once a person accepts God's grace through Christ in faith, his or her status changes from unholy to holy before God and from unacceptable to acceptable in God's presence.

Later in the same letter Paul explains that there was a time when his readers participated in sins unacceptable to God. They, however, had been *"washed, … sanctified, … justified in the name of the Lord Jesus Christ and by the Spirit of our God" (1 Cor. 6:11)*. God changed their status by cleansing them of their sins, making them holy before Him, and making them right according to His demands for righteousness.

In *Hebrews 10:10* the writer explained how Jesus' sacrifice of His life on the cross was God's final requirement for righteousness. It was *once for all.* Under the old covenant, God required people to make sacrifices to stay in right relationship with Him. The writer to the Hebrews explained that Jesus' death on the cross established a second and superior covenant. Jesus said His blood established this new covenant between God and people. (See *Matt. 26:27-28*.) Jesus' death on the cross completed God's demand for sacrifices to cover the sins of people. The result of the once-for-all sacrifice of Jesus was that "we have been made holy." His substitutionary death on your behalf fulfilled God's requirements for holiness. So, when God looks upon you after you have trusted Jesus as Lord and Savior, He no longer sees your sin. He sees His Son.

God makes you holy when you trust that Jesus Christ's death sufficiently fulfills God's demands for holiness for your life. The implications of this truth can change your life and how you see yourself. It has huge implications for your identity and how you describe yourself to others.

> *Sanctification is the process by which you are made holy; that is, acceptable by Holy God.*

✜ **Many Christians have never considered what it means to be declared completely acceptable by Holy God. Write some of the implications for your life and identity because God has declared you holy before Him.**

_____

_____

_____

_____

You Are Being Made Holy

The Bible also describes sanctification in the present tense. *Hebrews 10:14* states, *"because by one sacrifice he has made perfect forever those who are being made holy."* Again, the implication is that Jesus' sacrifice made those who believe perfectly acceptable to God, but it also expresses God's work of making one holy in the present tense. Is this a contradiction to the fact you are already holy in Christ? No. The verse describes another element of this process that changes your status before God. You have been made holy by Jesus' sacrifice, but you are also becoming holy in your daily living.

Remember the metaphor of a new birth to describe your relationship with God? When a child is born, genetically it has everything it needs to become an adult. The physical maturation process is the child becoming what its embedded genetic code says it will become. Apply the analogy to your spiritual life. When God makes you holy through Jesus and you receive new spiritual DNA, God places everything in your life you need to become a mature follower of Jesus. As you grow, you begin a spiritual maturation process to become what that embedded spiritual code has designed you to become. Part of that spiritual code is God's holiness. It is complete and present in your life just as adulthood is complete and present in the genetic code of a baby. Maturing in Christ is allowing God's holiness through Christ to grow to fullness in how you live.

Holy means *set apart.* In the Old Testament, God set apart an entire tribe to serve as priests *(Ex. 28). Holy* also implied living according to God's commands. In the Book of Leviticus, the command from God to *"be holy, because I am holy"* comes in the context of laws about what animals not to eat or touch *(Lev. 11:41-47).* Holiness had implications for daily living. God's people were to live lives set apart for Him. In the New Testament, *holy* continued to hold that same meaning. Peter called Christians a *holy priesthood,* signifying their special standing before God and their call to live separate lives for God *(1 Pet. 2:5).*

You are holy. Jesus' sacrifice made that happen. But, you are also becoming holy. You are becoming more like Jesus if you follow and obey Him. Just as a child becomes physically what its genetic code determines it to be, so you are to become spiritually what God's presence in your life has willed for you to be.

✦ **Examples in which God's holiness through Christ is expressed in my life include:**

_____

_____

_____

You Will Be Made Holy

Holiness is a past reality through your trust in Christ. Holiness is a present process of becoming like Jesus in your character and daily living. Sanctification also has a future aspect. While God sees you as holy through His Son, you cannot experience complete holiness in this life. That complete state of holiness can only be experienced in heaven. This is the future tense of being holy. Paul wrote to the Christians who asked about Christ's return, *"May he strengthen your hearts so that you will be blameless and holy in the presence of our God and Father when our Lord Jesus comes with all his holy ones" (1 Thess. 3:13).* Your holiness before God will be completed when you find yourself in His eternal presence.

✥ **Look at your description of sanctification. If your understanding of the word has changed, write a new description.**

_____
_____
_____
_____

SUMMARY

- The Bible uses the concept of sanctification in three tenses: past, present, and future.
- Once a person accepts God's grace through Christ in faith, his or her status changes from unholy to holy before God, unacceptable to acceptable in God's presence.
- God intends for His holiness to live itself out in your daily life. The more you live like Jesus, the more you will look like Jesus.
- Your holiness before God will be completed when you find yourself in the eternal presence of God.
- Jesus prayed to the Father that His followers be made holy by the truth of God's Word.

PERSONAL REFLECTION

✥ **Prayerfully complete these activities in your Identity Journal.**

1. **Being declared holy is the opposite of being declared an enemy of God. That is a huge change of status. Pause for a moment and thank God for His work of holiness in your life.**
2. **You are being made holy by God as you mature in your relationship with Him. Write three ways you sense you have become more holy in your choices and behaviors since you trusted Christ as your Savior. Take this opportunity to celebrate God's work in your life.**
3. **Is your life "set apart" for God's purposes? Explain.**
4. **How do you feel knowing that Jesus has prayed and is praying that you be holy as He is holy?**

MY STANDING WITH GOD

This week you will ...
- examine the biblical teaching that you are adopted into the family of God through trusting Jesus as the Son of God (Day 1);
- discover the implications of being an heir of God and the magnitude of your inheritance through Christ Jesus (Day 2);
- examine the biblical passages that explain the Holy Spirit's role in your standing with God (Day 3);
- examine your identity as a citizen of heaven and its implications for how you live (Day 4); and,
- examine the biblical image of your identity as a slave to righteousness and a slave of God (Day 5).

Memory Verse
You did not receive a spirit that makes you a slave again to fear, but you received the Spirit of sonship. And by him we cry, "Abba, Father" (Rom. 8:15).

ax Lucado tells the story of a king who traveled incognito to a nearby village. He had heard of the misfortune of five orphans, and he wanted to adopt them. When the orphans heard the king was coming, they began to work hard to impress him when he arrived—all but one little orphan. This little girl had no skill but the desire to care for people. She tried to learn what the other children were doing, but to no avail. She could only care for those who could not care for themselves.

When the king came to town dressed like a merchant, only the littlest orphan took time to care for him. She fed and brushed his donkey while he rested. When he awoke, the little girl stood by, simply enjoying his presence. He thanked her for her help and left. The king soon returned to find the little girl again. He explained that the other children were so busy preparing for his visit that they had no time to talk. Sometimes, he said, he just wanted to be their father, not the king they needed to impress. The king took the little girl to his castle, while the other children had to wait for a time when they were not so busy. Lucado ended his story: "And so it happened that the children with many talents but no time missed the visit of the king, while the girl whose only gift was her time to talk became his child."[1]

You have looked at your identity in Christ and the power of God's call on your life. You have discovered you have a spiritual DNA that causes dramatic changes in your behavior, and you have examined how your status with God has changed. This week's study will help you see the deep, loving relationship you have with God through Jesus Christ.

DAY 1
ADOPTED BY GOD

You did not receive a spirit that makes you a slave again to fear, but you received the Spirit of sonship. And by him we cry, "Abba, Father" (Rom. 8:15).

TODAY YOU WILL ...

❍ read the story of an adopted child;
❍ examine the biblical concept of adoption as a metaphor of your standing with God;
❍ review how your adoption relates to your identity in Christ; and,
❍ write a letter of thanks to God for adopting you as His child.

Brad and Kathy wanted children, but they could not have them naturally. As they began to pray, they concluded God's will for their lives was to adopt a child. They began the difficult process of adoption.

God led them to a child in an orphanage in Guatemala. When it was time to receive the child, they traveled to Central America. The adoption was delayed because of paperwork, and they could not find the child's mother. They waited there for over a month. To find the mother, they traveled to the end of a road and then walked to the mother's village. They tried three or four times to make contact, but she was never there when they arrived.

One hour before they had to go, the 14-year-old mother arrived. She was dressed in her native costume with decorative flowers in her hair. This was the first time she had seen her baby since she had given him life. She took the baby boy, walked to a corner, and spent a few minutes with her child. When she returned, she handed the baby to the boy's new mother. The interpreter asked if she had any last questions for her son's new parents. She paused, then asked, "Will he be with them forever?" Tears filled Kathy's eyes as she promised they would take care of him as long as they lived.

I will never forget the first time I saw Jake. His round face and big brown eyes framed in black hair made my eyes fill with tears. I knew the love that had motivated his parents to find him and bring him home. I knew what it had cost them to make the baby boy one of their family. When I called to ask Brad to recount this story for me, he said, "Just think, Gene, if we had gotten pregnant, we never would have had Jake. Now he's my boy!"

Jake's adoption by Brad and Kathy is a picture of your adoption by God. God chose you, traveled to your home village, waited for the right time, and adopted you into His family when you accepted His gracious offer. He even answered the question, "Will I be with Him forever?" Today's lesson is about your adoption into the family of God.

✦ **Do you know someone who adopted a child? Maybe you are adopted. What is their, or your, story? Be prepared to share your story at your next Identity Group meeting.**

You Are Adopted

Adoption is how you enter God's family. It is one more picture of your identity in Christ. You are adopted by the King of kings and share the privileges and rights of being a member of the royal family. Let's see how the Bible describes your relationship with God through adoption.

✦ **Read Romans 8:15-17. How does the Bible describe your standing with God?** _____
_____
_____

Having received the Spirit of sonship, what can you now do? _____
_____
_____

What does God's Spirit tell your spirit?_____
_____
_____

How does one's standing with God change after becoming a child of God? _____
_____
_____

> *You did not receive a spirit that makes you a slave again to fear, but you received the Spirit of sonship. And by him we cry, "Abba, Father." The Spirit himself testifies with our spirit that we are God's children. Now if we are children, then we are heirs—heirs of God and co-heirs with Christ, if indeed we share in his sufferings in order that we may also share in his glory (Rom. 8:15-17).*

The Bible contrasts your standing with God as being a slave filled with fear toward your master and being an adopted child who calls your new father, "Daddy." *(Abba* is an Aramaic word meaning *Father.* It is the familiar term used in the home.)[2]

God's Holy Spirit, reminds your spirit that you are a child of God. The implications of this adopted relationship are that as a child, you are an heir. And, if an heir, you are a coheir with Christ. You share in the inheritance of the very Son of God.

✠ **Read Galatians 4:4-7. When did God send His Son?** _____
_____

Why did God send His Son? _____
_____

What was the result of God's sending His Son? _____
_____
_____

What does God's Spirit do for the Christian? _____
_____
_____

What is your standing with God since God adopted you? _____
_____

> *But when the time had fully come, God sent his Son, born of a woman, born under law, to redeem those under law, that we might receive the full rights of sons. Because you are sons, God sent the Spirit who calls out "Abba, Father." So you are no longer a slave, but a son; and since you are a son, God has made you also an heir (Gal. 4:4-7).*

God sent His Son at just the right time, when God had moved all of history to receive Him. God sent Jesus to be born to a human woman under the old covenant laws so He could redeem (pay the price for) people under God's law. The result was that those who believe receive the full rights of sonship. God also sent His Spirit into our hearts so we can know the deep relationship of God as Father—even to the point of calling God "Daddy." In Christ, people are no longer slaves but children of God. If children, then heirs to God's kingdom.

The adoption language found in Romans and *Galatians 4:4-7* comes directly from the ancient adoption practices of that day. Slaves had no rights or privileges in the family that owned them. Masters were feared, and families were torn apart at his will. Sometimes, however, a master would choose to adopt a slave. When this happened, the slave received the same standing with the master as did his naturally born children. The slave-adopted-as-child received the same inheritance as the other children. Adoption meant one was "granted the full rights and privileges of sonship in a family to which one does not belong by nature."[3] It is paying a price of love so a slave can become a son.

God inspired Paul to use this common practice to describe how a Christian's status changes before God. In addition, this new status before God provides a new standing with God. You can know God personally and have a deep, loving relationship with the God who created you and loves you. To help you in your new relationship, God gives you His Holy Spirit so you can know God as intimately as children can know their loving father. He is not just "Father." He can be known as "Daddy." Only children of the Father can call Him Daddy.

So, What Does That Make Me?

Before you trusted Christ, you were a slave to sin, an object of God's wrath. You had no rights in the family of God, and you feared God. While you were a sinner, God demonstrated His love for you by sending His Son to pay the price for your adoption. All you had to do was accept His gift of adoption, and you were in God's family. After your confession of faith, God adopted you as His child with full rights of membership in His family. You were no longer a slave. You were the son or daughter of the God who created you.

What does this make you? What is your identity in Christ? You are a full-fledged child of God, adopted with the price paid by Jesus' death on the cross. God loved you so much He sent His Son to die a cruel death to pay the price of your adoption. He searched for you and promised you would live with Him forever. You are worth the cost of God's Son. You are a child of the King.

A Letter of Thanks

When I was a youth minister, we had as many as six adopted children in our youth group. Occasionally, I would ask one of them to tell his or her story and what it meant to be adopted. I remember one student who told of how he found out who his biological mother and father were. He told how he was thankful his mother had not aborted him, but sad he did not know her—until he remembered who his adoptive parents were. They had done so much for him and loved him as their own. He thanked God he had been adopted. Other students would tell their stories. Some would read letters of thanks they had written to their adopting parents.

In your Identity Journal or on a separate sheet of paper, write a letter of thanks to God for adopting you into His family. You may want to tell of your life before your adoption. You may want to tell God how much you appreciate His seeking you out and paying the ultimate price of His Son's death so you could be in His family. You will be asked to share your letter with your Identity Group at the next session.

SUMMARY

- Adoption is how you enter the family of God. It is another picture of your identity in Christ.
- The Bible contrasts your standing with God as a slave filled with fear toward your master and an adopted child who calls your new father "Daddy."
- After your confession of faith, God adopted you as His child with full rights of membership in His family.
- You are worth the cost of God's Son. You are a child of the King.

PERSONAL REFLECTION

⊕ **Prayerfully complete these activities in your Identity Journal.**

1. Think of the biblical truths of how you come into relationship with God. Which one so far is your favorite? Why?
2. Write your impressions of God before you were a Christian. Were they positive or negative? Did they match the phrase a slave again to fear?
3. How does the phrase, by him we cry, "Abba [or 'Daddy'], Father" change your understanding about your relationship with God? Does calling God "Daddy" seem right to you?
4. The Bible states you are a child—if a child, then an heir. Since you are an heir, you are a coheir with Christ. How does this help you understand your identity in Christ? What implications does this have for how you live your life?

[1]From *Tell Me the Story* by Max Lucado, illustrated by Ron DiCianni, © 1992, pps. 24-29. Used by permission of Crossway Books, a division of Good News Publishers, Wheaton, Illinois 60187. This story is also available as a picture book titled *Just the Way You Are,* illustrated by Sergio Martinez. Either book may be ordered from Crossway Books at 1-800-635-7993.
[2]Leon Morris, *The Epistle to the Romans* (Grand Rapids: William B. Eerdmans Publishing Company, 1988), 315.
[3]Ibid.

DAY 2

IF ADOPTED, THEN AN HEIR!

Now if we are children, then we are heirs—
heirs of God and co-heirs with Christ, if
indeed we share in his sufferings in order
that we may also share in his glory
(Rom. 8:17).

TODAY YOU WILL ...

○ write your ideas of what you would do with a portion of a $58 billion dollar inheritance;
○ understand that you are an heir in Christ;
○ examine the truth of your inheritance as God's child; and,
○ describe how your life would be if you trusted the truth of God's Word about your standing with Him and the inheritance He has promised you.

Imagine you were the child of Bill Gates, founder of Microsoft. In 1998 his personal worth was $58 billion dollars.[1] That's right. I said *illion* with a *B*. Since you are a legitimate child, you are an heir to his estate.

🕀 **What would you do if you knew you had access to those kinds of resources? Write in the margin how you would live and what you would do knowing that much money was potentially in your future. Be prepared to share answers with your Identity Group.**

If a Child, then an Heir

In the last session you discovered God has declared your standing with Him as an adopted child. In this session you will examine the implications of your new identity in Christ. Let's return to Paul's letter to the

Romans. He declared that you did not receive a spirit of fear but the *Spirit of sonship (Rom. 8:15)*. You are a child of God through God's work of adoption in Christ Jesus. So, what does that mean?

⊕ **Reread Romans 8:17 (p. 102) and fill in the blanks below.**

Now if we are _____, then we are _____–_____ of God and _____ with Christ (Rom. 8:17).

You can also translate the word *if* at the beginning of the verse with *since* (NLT). It would read, *Since we are children, then we are also heirs.* Based on the fact that God has adopted you, your standing with Him becomes that of His heir. Not only that, but you become a coheir with Christ, God's only Son (as opposed to God's adopted children).

The image is vivid. You are an outsider trapped in sin. God loves you so much He chooses to adopt you. He pays the price of adoption with the sacrifice of His only born Son. This payment frees you from slavery to sin. You become God's child. Now that you are a child of God, God informs you that your new position makes you His heir and coheir with His only-born, resurrected Son, Jesus Christ. (And you thought being Bill Gates' child offered you resources!)

The truth of being an heir of God is biblically significant. It is not just a way to help you understand your identity. It is a primary picture of how a person receives God's promised inheritance of salvation.

⊕ **Read Galatians 3:15-29 in your Bible.**

How do you become a child of God? (v. 25-26)
○ **Through keeping the law**   ○ **By faith in Christ Jesus?**

What happens to the differences between people once they find their new standing with God? (v. 28) _____
_____
_____

What is Paul's conclusion to his argument in verse 29? What is the significance of being an heir? _____
_____
_____

You become a child of God through trusting Christ, not by keeping the law *(vv. 26-27)*. No differences exist between those who have been adopted into the family of God *(v. 28)*. Since you now belong to God's family, you are part of Abraham's seed and heirs according to the original promise. In Christ, you are an heir to the promise God made Abraham—a relationship with Christ. Being an heir to this inheritance makes you part of God's work since the beginning of time.

> "We ourselves ... groan inwardly as we wait eagerly for our adoption as sons, the redemption of our bodies" (Rom. 8:28).

> I pray also that the eyes of your heart may be enlightened in order that you may know the hope to which he has called you, the riches of his glorious inheritance in the saints (Eph. 1:18).

> Giving thanks to the Father, who has qualified you to share in the inheritance of the saints in the kingdom of light (Col. 1:12).

⊕ **Record your feelings and impressions about being an heir of God's ancient promise. What implications does this have for your identity in Christ? Write your responses in your Identity Journal.**

As with sanctification, you will not experience your full adoption until you are in eternity with God. Just as Brad and Kathy's son was adopted but not in his new home while still in Guatemala, so you are adopted but do not experience the full implications of being God's adopted child until you are at your new home in heaven. (See *Rom. 8:28.*)

If an Heir, Then an Inheritance

Jesus Christ was the promised inheritance to Abraham. Those who have trusted in Christ have also become heirs to that promise. But, you may ask, "Is there more to my inheritance?" The answer is, "Yes!" While a relationship with God through Christ is enough, the Bible describes your inheritance in other ways. Let's take a look at some of them.

⊕ **Read the passages in the margin and underline words or short phrases that describe your inheritance as an heir of God.**

Paul began his letter to the Ephesians with a prayer that they would know (1) the hope to which God had called them; (2) the riches of his glorious inheritance in the saints; and (3) God's incomparable great power for those who trust Him. *The riches of his glorious inheritance in the saints (Eph. 1:18)* describes the wealth and glory of your inheritance. Pray that you may be enlightened about this truth.

God inspired Paul to write to the Christians in Colossae to give thanks to the Father, *who has qualified you to share in the inheritance of the saints in the kingdom of light (Col. 1:12).* Through your adoption by God you are qualified to take part in the inheritance of those who belong to the kingdom of light. Like the little orphan in Lucado's story, you will go home with the King and enjoy all the wealth, rights, and privileges of being part of the Royal Family.

⊕ **Describe your inheritance as an heir of God. Include your feelings about how this truth affects your understanding of your identity in Christ. Write your thoughts in your Identity Journal and be prepared to share in your Identity Group.**

How Can You Say No?

I love reading John Grisham novels. *The Testament* is the story of a lawyer hired by the estate of a billionaire to find and inform its heir that she will receive the entire estate. The lawyer finds the heir serving as a missionary to an obscure native tribe in Brazil. When she finds time to talk with him, he informs her of her newfound wealth. All she has to do is sign some papers, and she is a multi-billionaire. At this point in the story you wonder, *How is her life going to change from being a missionary in the far reaches of civilization to being on the Forbes list of the 400 Richest People in America?* Her first response is that she does not want the money. Nate, the lawyer, is surprised. You have to wonder how anyone could say no to such an unbelievable amount of money and status—without doing anything but being someone's child and signing some papers. She would be set for life!

You will have to read the book to see what happens, but the question is a real one: *How can anyone say no to such an inheritance?* Apply this question to God's promised inheritance to anyone who puts his or her trust in Jesus Christ. How can anyone say no to the riches and glory that come from being heir to the God of the Universe?

✚ Write the name of a person who needs this inheritance.

_____

_____

Have you told this person of the inheritance of God's promise? Why has he or she refused it? What is he or she valuing more than accepting a standing with God as heir and coheir with Christ? _____

_____

_____

SUMMARY

- Based on the fact that God has adopted you, your standing with Him becomes that of an heir.
- You are a coheir with His only-born, resurrected Son, Jesus Christ.
- You become a child of God by trusting Christ, not keeping the law.
- The question to answer is "How can anyone say no to such an inheritance?"

PERSONAL REFLECTION

✚ Prayerfully complete these activities in your Identity Journal.

1. **What is it about great wealth that causes people to get excited? If you had to choose between Bill Gate's wealth and your inheritance through Christ, which would you choose?**
2. **If you were an heir of a rich and famous person, how would it affect your sense of security and identity? Apply the same question to yourself as an heir of God.**
3. **What are some reasons people refuse the spiritual wealth of God's inheritance? How could you help them to accept God's promise?**

---

[1]John Gorham, Peter Kafka, and Shailaja Neelakantan, "The Richest People in America," *Forbes Magazine*, <http://forbes.com/forbes/98/1012/6208165a.htm> (12 October 1998).

DAY 3

THE HOLY SPIRIT

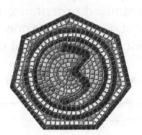

"You also were included in Christ when you heard the word of truth, the gospel of your salvation. Having believed, you were marked in him with a seal, the promised Holy Spirit, who is a deposit guaranteeing our inheritance until the redemption of those who are God's possession—to the praise of his glory" (Eph. 1:13-14).

TODAY YOU WILL ...

○ recall a time you purchased an expensive item and made a deposit to ensure your purchase;
○ examine the biblical evidence for the Holy Spirit's part in guaranteeing your eternal inheritance;
○ discover ways the Holy Spirit helps you in the transformational process of becoming like Jesus; and,
○ examine Jesus' teachings about the character of a Christian.

Have you ever walked into a store and seen something you really wanted, but didn't have enough money to buy it? What did you do? Your commitment to Christ eliminates stealing as an option. You still have a couple of other ways to get what you want. One option is to put the item on "hold" until you can return with more money. This, however, doesn't guarantee someone else won't buy it before you get back. Another option is to make a down payment or put it on "lay away" with the money that you do have. Giving partial amount of the money guarantees you will be back to buy the item. The store is obligated to hold the item for a reasonable amount of time until you return with the rest of the money. This money can be called a down payment or earnest money.

⊕ **When was the last time you purchased an item that required a down payment or earnest money? Record that experience in the margin and share it in your next Identity Group meeting.**

God's "Earnest Money"

God has adopted you through His Son. Your standing with God is that of an heir, even a coheir with Christ. What assurances do you have that you will receive your inheritance? Although you have no right to ask for assurances any more than the right to be adopted in the first place, God has freely offered you an assurance of His promises.

⊕ **Reread Ephesians 1:13-14 (p. 110). What two metaphors describe the Holy Spirit in your life? Write your answers below.**

1. _____
2. _____

The Bible teaches that from the time you first believed, you were *included in Christ.* It is in that relationship that you were *marked in him with a seal,* which is the Holy Spirit. A seal in the ancient world could mean a mark of identification that denoted ownership. "A seal could also mean the mark of a person on a document that confirmed or authenticated that document."[1] The seal of God's presence in the believer is the Holy Spirit. It is evidence that you belong to God's family.

The second image for the Holy Spirit is a deposit or earnest money. This deposit guaranteeing our inheritance is the same idea as the down payment or, earnest money I described in the opening story. The word was used in the ancient world to mean a *"first installment, deposit, down payment, pledge,* that pays a part of the purchase price in advance, and so secures a legal claim to the article in question, or makes a contract valid."[2] God has said by giving you His Holy Spirit that you belong to Him and that you will receive your inheritance—guaranteed!

The Work of the Holy Spirit

Let's apply those two pictures to your life. First, the seal of the Holy Spirit is God's mark of ownership on your life. How do you know you are a child of God? How can you be certain God's promise of your inheritance is true? God said His Holy Spirit in you seals His promise to you. How does the Holy Spirit "seal" you?

Jesus promised He would send the Spirit of God to His followers when He returned to heaven *(John 16:13,15).* The seal of the Holy Spirit in your life will help you accept the truth of who you are as an heir of God's riches. It is the mark that says you are God's child.

The Holy Spirit can also be a seal of authenticity. How do you know something is the real deal? Many people wanted hockey souvenirs when the Dallas Stars won the Stanley Cup in 1999. T-shirts, hats, jerseys, and pucks became coveted items. As you would expect, items such as jerseys began to appear that looked authentic but were not.

111

Neither the Stars nor the NHL sanctioned the products. How did you know you were getting the real thing? The authentic jerseys and other souvenirs had a seal manufactured by the sanctioning organizations. Only those with the three-dimensional NHL seal were the real deal.

So, what do authentic NHL souvenirs have to do with your identity in Christ? The Bible states the Holy Spirit is God's seal of authenticity in your life. His presence tells others you are the real deal. So, How can others see the Holy Spirit in you? One way others see the Holy Spirit in you and the way you know God is present in your life is what the Bible calls the fruit of the Spirit. Fruit is a picture word for evidence of God's presence.

> **The fruit of the Spirit is love, joy, peace, patience, kindness, goodness, faithfulness, gentleness, and self-control. Against such things there is no law (Gal. 5:22-23).**

✦ **Read Galatians 5:22-23 and explain in your own words how these characteristics of Christ in your life could be evidence of God's Spirit in your life.** _____
_____
_____
_____

The presence of God's Holy Spirit in your life is not just assurance you belong to God. Another picture is that He is God's down payment that you will receive your inheritance of salvation. The Holy Spirit is God's "deposit" that guarantees your inheritance of salvation. This down payment is God's promise that you will and can become like Jesus. Just as the fruit of God's Spirit signals His presence to others and to you, you will begin to see other evidences of the Holy Spirit's work in your life. Your character, your worldview, and your appetite will change.

God's deposit of His Holy Spirit in your life is a guarantee you can develop the character of Christ in your life. If God's Spirit lives in your life, you can expect He will influence every aspect of your life. We will explore more about this in next week's study. Know now that as an adopted child of God, sealed with God's Holy Spirit, your life will begin to show evidences of God's presence in your life—guaranteed!

SUMMARY

- While you have no right to ask for assurances any more than you have a right to be adopted in the first place, God has freely offered you an assurance of His promises.
- The seal of God's presence in the believer is the Holy Spirit. It is evidence that you belong to God's family.
- God's Holy Spirit in your life is His "deposit" that makes certain you will receive the promised inheritance.
- The Bible states the Holy Spirit is God's seal of authenticity in your life. His presence tells others you are the real deal.

PERSONAL REFLECTION

⊕ **Prayerfully complete these activities in your Identity Journal.**

1. **If someone came up to you and demanded proof that you are your father's child, what document would you show? If asked for proof you are God's child, what evidence could you show?**
2. **The Holy Spirit is a mark of God's ownership in your life. How can this truth help you when you doubt who you are in Christ?**
3. **Complete the following "guarantee" of your standing with God: "I have been guaranteed I am an heir of God's riches because ..."**

---

[1]Johannes P. Louw and Eugene A. Nida, eds., *Greek-English Lexicon of the New Testament Based on Semantic Domains, Vol. 1* (New York: United Bible Societies, 1988), 804.

[2]Ibid., 109.

DAY 4

A CITIZEN OF HEAVEN

Consequently, you are no longer foreigners and aliens, but fellow citizens with God's people and members of God's household (Eph. 2:19).

TODAY YOU WILL ...

○ express your feelings about visiting a foreign country;
○ examine the biblical analogy of citizenship as part of your identity in Christ;
○ compare Paul's images of being strangers and aliens with being a citizen with God's people; and,
○ apply the fact that you are a citizen of heaven to how you live.

My first trip to another continent was to Russia. A group from our church traveled to St. Petersburg to help equip Christians to rebuild the ministries of the church after 70 years of Communist domination. This was not long after the wall had been brought down in East Berlin and Russia had moved to a more capitalistic economy. The country was still unstable as to what its future would be. The Christians there were warm and accepting. We were brothers and sisters in Christ and shared a citizenship in heaven. But, we were also citizens from different countries. I remember when we pulled up on the runway the first day there that Russian troops surrounded the plane. That was new for me. I also remember seeing more military personnel than ever before on the streets and in the buildings of the city. We even had talked with our host about plans to leave the city in case the Communist Party tried to regain control. By the end of the week, however, we felt at ease with our Christian brothers and sisters, but we also knew where the United States Embassy was located! I was never so pleased to come home to my home country than after that first trip away.

⊕ **Have you ever traveled to another country? How did you feel? What precautions did you take to protect your passport? Plan to share your feelings in your Identity Group.**

Your Citizenship

Another picture of your standing with God and your identity is citizenship. You identify yourself as a citizen of the United States of America or another country. That identity travels with you wherever you go. It is the basis of the freedoms you enjoy in your home country.

Being a citizen of a country gives you protection by that country and the rights and privileges afforded you by that country's laws. If you travel, you can find help from your country's embassy in the host country. Citizenship means you depend on that country to protect you from invaders and civil disruptions. You also depend on your country to provide services for you and your family. That is, of course, if those governing are respecters of persons and the law of the land.

Citizenship was important in ancient times, too. In the first century, Roman citizenship was greatly desired. Rome ruled the ancient world, and being a citizen offered a person several rights and privileges. We know that a Roman citizen could not be flogged without a trial. (See *Acts 22:22-29*.) We also know that a Roman citizen could appeal his case directly to Caesar himself. (See *Acts 25:10*.) Paul took advantage of his Roman citizenship to further God's call on his life.

When Paul wrote to the Christians in Ephesus, he used the analogy of citizenship to describe how non-Jewish people share in the benefits of being citizens in the true Israel.

⊕ **Read Ephesians 2:11-22 in your Bible. How did Paul describe the condition of the non-Jewish people?** _____
_____
_____

How did that change when they became "in Christ Jesus"? _____

_____

_____

What word (used four times in vv. 14-18) signifies the work of Christ among the people of the world? _____

How did Paul describe non-Jewish people who had trusted Christ?

_____

_____

Paul explained that Jews saw the non-Jewish people, Gentiles, as *separate from Christ, excluded from citizenship in Israel and foreigners to the covenants of the promise (v. 12)*. Gentiles were incapable of holding citizenship among God's people. How could that change? *Verse 13* states, *"But now in Christ Jesus you who once were far away have been brought near through the blood of Christ."* Jesus is the peace (mentioned four times in *vv. 14-18*) that breaks down the division between those who have access to God's promises and those who cannot access God's covenant love by birth. Jesus created a way for all to *have access to the Father by one Spirit (v. 18)*. Paul, then, came to the heart of his illustration. *Ephesians 2:19* is our verse for the day. Read it again in the margin. Observe the word pictures that describe how one's standing with God changes through a relationship with Jesus.

Paul said, *"You are no longer foreigners and aliens."* In the ancient world, a foreigner was basically an enemy because he was unknown and feared to be sinister.[1] If you put English letters in place of the original Greek letters, you get the root word for *xenophobia,* a fear of foreigners. An alien, on the other hand, was one who lived among resident citizens of a country without having any rights of citizenship. These aliens, however, received the protection from those with whom they lived.[2] Paul taught that in Christ Jesus those who were seen as foreigners and aliens before were no longer viewed as outsiders.

He then said that they were *fellow citizens with God's people and members of God's household (v. 19)*. Paul also described the church as *God's household, which is the church of the living God (1 Tim. 3:15)*. What a change! Through Christ people are no longer outsiders to be feared or simply considered neighbors. They have gained a new standing in the community. They are citizens with the others who live with them. They have the same rights and privileges as naturally-born citizens. They are also members of the family. A relationship with Christ makes the foreigner a citizen and the alien a member of the family.

The place of your citizenship is part of your identity in Christ. Paul taught the Philippians, *Our citizenship is in heaven. And we eagerly await a Savior from there, the Lord Jesus Christ (Phil. 3:20)*. Based on the teachings of Scripture, you have dual citizenship. You belong to two countries—one natural and physical, the other spiritual.

> *Consequently, you are no longer foreigners and aliens, but fellow citizens with God's people and members of God's household (Eph. 2:19).*

⊕ **Complete the following sentences.**

Naturally, or through naturalization, I am a citizen of ... _____

_____

Spiritually, through my relationship with Jesus, I am a citizen of ...
_____

Where should your ultimate allegiance be? What rights and privileges can you count on? Which will ultimately be more significant? _____

_____

We have said, "Whose you are determines who you are." Let me add, "Where your citizenship is determines where your loyalties lie." Your standing with God is that of an adopted child and a citizen of heaven. Both of those realities should encourage you as you trust who you are in Christ and where your home really is.

SUMMARY

- Another picture of your standing with God is citizenship.
- A relationship with Christ makes the foreigner a citizen and the alien a member of the family.
- The place of your citizenship is part of your identity in Christ.
- Being a citizen of heaven not only has implications for your identity, but it also impacts how you live in your home country.

PERSONAL REFLECTION

⊕ **Prayerfully complete these activities in your Identity Journal.**

1. **Have you ever known someone who came to this country and became a citizen? If so, ask him or her what it felt like moving into the community. Ask how he or she felt as a stranger and about the first person to show them kindness.**
2. **Make two columns in your Identity Journal. In the left-hand column, list some of the benefits of being a citizen of your country. In the right-hand column list the benefits you have by being a citizen of heaven. How do the two compare?**
3. **Answer the question, If an unbeliever came into my home and stayed with my family for a day, in what ways would they know our ultimate citizenship was in heaven?**

_____

[1]Colin Brown, ed., *The New International Dictionary of New Testament Theology*, (Zondervan, 1975), 686.
[2]Ibid.,687.

DAY 5

A SERVANT OF GOD

"Now that you have been set free from sin and have become slaves to God, the benefit you reap leads to holiness, and the result is eternal life" (Rom. 6:22).

TODAY YOU WILL ...

○ review previously discussed pictures of your standing with God;
○ examine the biblical image of being a slave to righteousness;
○ review how biblical writers saw themselves as servants of God; and,
○ examine the concept of being a servant to God's call.

✦ **Record one truth from each lesson that describes your standing with God. Record a passage of Scripture that supports each reality**

Day 1: _____

Day 2: _____

Day 3: _____

Day 4: _____

This week you have seen four pictures of your standing with God: (1) You are an adopted child *(Rom. 8:15)*. (2) You are an heir and eligible to receive an eternal inheritance *(Rom. 8:17)*. (3) The Holy Spirit is God's guarantee that you will receive His promised inheritance *(Eph. 1:13-14)*. (4) You are a citizen of heaven *(1 Pet. 1:17; 2:11)*.

✦ **Reflect on which of those truths has most changed your perception of your standing before God. Complete the statement, "My perception of my standing with God has changed because I learned that in Christ I am ..." Record your response in your Identity Journal. Be prepared to share your thoughts with your Identity Group.**

A Slave to Righteousness

Slavery is not a picture you would naturally choose to describe your standing with God. Slavery of a human by another is wrong. So, how can such an image help you understand your identity in Christ? Let's return to the letter to the Romans and see if we can follow Paul's teaching to the Christians there.

⊕ **Read Romans 6:15-23 in your Bible. Who does Paul say you are a slave to?** _____

_____

What is the result of being a slave to sin? to obedience? _____

_____

_____

What have you become by being set free from sin? _____

_____

To what does the Bible invite you to offer the parts of your body?

_____

_____

What else have you become by being set free from sin? _____

_____

What are your wages as a slave to sin? What is the alternative to those wages? _____

_____

The Bible explains how you are a slave to righteousness and to God. First, it teaches the truth that you become a slave to those you choose to obey *(Rom. 6:16)*. The Bible states you either serve sin or righteousness. The one you choose becomes your master and you its slave. Choosing which one to serve also determines where you will end up. Slavery to sin leads to death. Slavery to obedience leads to righteousness. You naturally chose to be enslaved by sin, but you have been set free from that master in Christ. Your freedom from sin allows you to become a slave to righteousness *(Rom. 6:18)*. You are also a slave of God because of your freedom from sin. (See *Rom. 6:22*.)

Writing in terms everyone could understand, Paul taught that you should offer the parts of your body to righteousness rather than to sin. This teaching reminds us of how physical disciplines can produce spiritual growth. If you commit your body to righteousness, the result is holiness *(Rom. 6:19)*. This result is the ongoing reality of sanctification. Your daily choices to serve the things of God will transform you into the likeness of Jesus.

Some slaves received wages for their work. If you are a slave to sin, then your wage at the end of your life is death. On the other hand, God offers you a gift of eternal life in Christ Jesus. That gift frees you from the slavery of sin and allows you to choose righteousness as your master.

You may have never thought of your standing with God as that of a slave. You would prefer to be free. But the Bible teaches these two truths: you tend to enslave yourself to something or someone, and you cannot serve two masters at the same time.

⊕ **What things or people do you tend to make masters over your life? Could you call yourself a "slave" to anything? Are you a slave to sin or to righteousness? Write your responses in the margin. (You will be asked to share this in confidence with one of your Identity Group members at the next meeting.)**

The Bible clearly teaches the consequences of what you choose to obey. Sin results in death. Righteousness results in holiness. In Christ Jesus, you can be set free from sin and death so you can become a slave to righteousness.

A Servant to God's Mission

The apostle Paul did not hesitate to call himself a servant of Christ. You see this in the introductions of his letters *(Rom. 1:1; Phil. 1:1; Titus 1:1)*. By identifying himself as a servant of Christ, he declared that he belonged to Jesus and that Jesus was his Lord. Paul also proclaimed that he had become a servant to the church. This did not come by choice, but by call.

⊕ **Read Colossians 1:24-25. Summarize how Paul describes his relationship to the church?** _____

Paul said that he rejoiced in his sufferings on behalf of his readers. His trials were for the sake of Christ's body, which is the church. Paul announced that he had become a servant to the church because of God's co-mission with him to share the gospel with all peoples. Paul said he had become a servant due to God's call. In response, Paul humbled himself to God's mission for his life. He was to serve the church in order to tell others about Jesus. He became a servant leader.

"A servant leader serves the mission and leads by serving those on mission with him."[1] Paul became a servant to God's mission for his life. He led by serving others who had joined him on that mission. God's call became Paul's passion, and that passion became his life. God's mission became the only goal for his life. Paul passionately served that mission after God made his call clear.

You, too, can become a servant leader. If you will humble yourself to God's call on your life, you can know the same purpose and joy of being known as a servant of God, a servant leader.

You are an adopted child who is an heir of God. God has guaranteed your inheritance with the down payment of His Holy Spirit. You are a citizen of heaven and a servant of God.

Now I rejoice in what was suffered for you, and I fill up in my flesh what is still lacking in regard to Christ's afflictions, for the sake of his body, which is the church. I have become its servant by the commission God gave me to present to you the word of God in its fullness (Col. 1:24-25).

SUMMARY

- The Bible explains how you are a slave to righteousness and to God.
- Choosing what to serve also determines where you will end up. Slavery to sin leads to death. Slavery to obedience leads to righteousness.
- In Christ Jesus, you can be set free from sin and death so you can become a slave to righteousness.
- By saying they were servants of God, New Testament writers also said, God is our Master. Another way to say this is, I belong to Jesus Christ.
- If you will humble yourself to God's call on your life, you can know the same purpose and joy of being known as a servant of God.

PERSONAL REFLECTION

⊕ **Prayerfully complete these activities in your Identity Journal.**

1. **The biblical image of being a slave to anything may be foreign to your thinking. List reasons why you would naturally resist considering yourself a slave to anything or anyone.**
2. **The Bible instructs you to offer [the parts of your body] in slavery to righteousness leading to holiness (Rom. 6:19). What are some practical ways you can do this?**
3. **The biblical writers identified themselves as servants of Christ Jesus. If you were to identify yourself at the beginning of a letter, how would you describe yourself? How could you write "servant of God" another way to capture the same meaning?**
4. **Could you be called a servant leader? Have you humbled yourself to God's purposes for your life? Are you comfortable being known as a servant of God?**

---

[1]From *Jesus on Leadership* by C. Gene Wilkes, © 1998 LifeWay Press. Used by permission of Tyndale House Publishers, Inc. All rights reserved.

WEEK 6

MY WAY OF LIFE

This week you will ...
○ discover the secret of how change happens in your life (Day 1);
○ learn what it means to be an "apprentice to Jesus" (Day 2);
○ examine ways you can prepare your life for spiritual transformation (Day 3);
○ examine practices that allow God to grow fruit in your life (Day 4); and,
○ review the implications of your identity in Christ (Day 5).

Memory Verse
"By their fruit you will recognize them. Do people pick grapes from thornbushes, or figs from thistles? Likewise every good tree bears good fruit, but a bad tree bears bad fruit. A good tree cannot bear bad fruit, and a bad tree cannot bear good fruit" (Matt. 7:16-18).

You may have heard of Cassie Bernall. She was the Columbine High School student who said "yes" when asked if she believed in God by two shooters. Her answer cost her her life. Cassie's "unlikely martyrdom" did not come after trusting Jesus at an early age. In her story written by her mother, *She Said Yes,* Mrs. Bernall tells how Cassie had connected with a girl who told Cassie to kill her parents. The Bernalls were frightened by the suggestion. They pulled Cassie out of the school, refused her contact with that group of friends, and made her begin attending church. Cassie, as you would guess, was not happy with her parents' decisions. She resisted, but eventually followed their direction. Mrs. Bernall tells what happened when Cassie went on a retreat with the church youth group in Estes Park, Colorado. There Cassie made her commitment to Christ. When she returned from the retreat, all Cassie told her mother was, "Mom, I've changed. I've totally changed. I know you are not going to believe it, but I'll prove it to you." Two years later, Cassie died for her faith. On the morning of April 20, 1999, Cassie gave a note to her friend Amanda. The PS read, "Honestly, I want to live completely for God. It's hard and scary, but totally worth it."

Her life following the experience proved she had changed. Madeline L'engle wrote in the forward to Cassie's story, "Cassie could not have answered that question if she had not already asked it of herself many times and answered Yes many times." Cassie could say yes that day because it was part of her relationship with God.[1]

---
[1]Taken from Misty Bernall, *She Said Yes* (Farmington: The Plough Publishing House, Copyright © 1999), xiii, 82-83.

DAY 1

FRUIT, NOT EFFORT

" 'I am the vine; you are the branches. If a man remains in me and I in him, he will bear much fruit; apart from me you can do nothing' " (John 15:5).

TODAY YOU WILL ...

○ read about one person's struggle to change his emotions;
○ discover the secret for change in your life;
○ examine Jesus' teaching on how fruit is produced in your life; and,
○ examine how the Bible describes your relationship with Jesus.

Jason (not his real name) had a group of friends he spent most of his time with—especially on the weekends. Jason grew up in the church and knew the difference between right and wrong, too. He hung out with his friends every weekend. One night, the group decided to meet some other students to drink. Jason had promised himself he would never drink, but everyone else was drinking so he joined in. He went more and more often to meet his friends. He still went to church, but it got harder and harder to go every week. Eventually, he stopped going to church. He wanted to stop drinking, but couldn't. He was afraid of losing his friends. There's a Jason (or Jackie) in every youth group. They may even call themselves Christians but can't seem to change once they start hanging with a certain group. Change seems impossible—no matter how hard they try or how much they want to.

You may have a similar struggle with friends and/or circumstances in your life. It may be as serious as giving up your Christian commitments or as simple as wanting to create a new habit in your life. Write your struggle in the margin. Share it with someone and ask him or her to pray for you.

The Secret to Change

Christianity is not a self-help course. The secret to change is not through your efforts, but through God's work in your life. Change is the result of who you are in Christ, not what you do for Christ. Many Christians have bought into the myth that effort alone somehow affects their standing before God. They seem to think, or have been taught, that if they just try harder, things will get better. But, Jesus never told people to try harder. Yes, He told His followers how to live, but all of those instructions were built on a personal relationship with Him first. Jesus always began by inviting people to follow Him. The follower initiated change only as it related to coming to Jesus; that is, repentance. Once a person submitted himself to Jesus as Lord, he learned to live according to God's design. Conformity to God's image came as a result of a relationship with Christ.

You may say, Wrong! Gene, I can quote you 50 verses that tell me to do something because I am a Christian. For example, you already quoted Paul's instruction to *set your mind on things above (Col. 3:2)*. The Bible does have many instructions that seem to be efforts on your part. Paul said to set your mind on things above *since ... you have been raised with Christ (Col. 3:1)*. You don't set your mind on things above in order to be raised with Christ. The order is—since you have been raised with Christ, set your mind on things above.

If you start with the action before building the relationship, you end up with nothing but religious activity. On the other hand, if you develop your relationship with Christ first, then the activity of your life will begin to show the effects of that relationship. In other words, relationship precedes effort to live a life worthy of your calling. Any effort on your part is simply in response to your relationship with God.

It's the Fruit, Not the Effort

Jesus taught that your actions are the result of who you are. He used a common analogy—fruit produced by a plant or tree—to explain the basis for living as He commanded.

Read Matthew 7:15-20. Based on the location of this text in Matthew, what is the context of Jesus' statement?
○ **Teaching in the temple area**
○ **Sermon on the Mount**
○ **Instruction by the Sea of Galilee**

How did Jesus say you can recognize a true prophet?
○ **The way he dresses**
○ **The manner in which he talks**
○ **By his fruit—the way he acts**

What was the truth Jesus taught with His analogy about good trees and bad trees? _____

> *"Watch out for false prophets. They come to you in sheep's clothing, but inwardly they are ferocious wolves. By their fruit you will recognize them. Do people pick grapes from thornbushes, or figs from thistles? Likewise every good tree bears good fruit, but a bad tree bears bad fruit. A good tree cannot bear bad fruit, and a bad tree cannot bear good fruit. Every tree that does not bear good fruit is cut down and thrown into the fire. Thus, by their fruit you will recognize them"* (Matt. 7:15-20).

> "I am the true vine, and my Father is the gardener. He cuts off every branch in me that bears no fruit, while every branch that does bear fruit he prunes so that it will be even more fruitful. You are already clean because of the word I have spoken to you. Remain in me, and I will remain in you. No branch can bear fruit by itself; it must remain in the vine. Neither can you bear fruit unless you remain in me.
>
> "I am the vine; you are the branches. If a man remains in me and I in him, he will bear much fruit; apart from me you can do nothing. If anyone does not remain in me, he is like a branch that is thrown away and withers; such branches are picked up, thrown into the fire and burned. If you remain in me and my words remain in you, ask whatever you wish, and it will be given you. This is to my Father's glory, that you bear much fruit, showing yourselves to be my disciples" (John 15:1-8).

How do you know who someone really is? _____
_____
_____

The context for Jesus' teaching about fruit is His Sermon on the Mount *(Matt. 5—7)*. He taught His followers to tell whether a person was a true prophet by the fruit of his or her life, how he or she acted. Jesus said that His creation taught this truth. Only grapevines bear grapes and fig trees bear figs. You can't get those results from thornbushes and thistles. It's a fact of nature that good, or healthy, trees bear good fruit, and bad, or unhealthy trees, bear bad fruit. So it is with people. Those who are spiritually unhealthy are only capable of bad fruit, and they will be cut down and thrown into the fire. Jesus said that you know people by their actions. What they do will always tell who they really are.

✚ **Read John 15:1-8. What analogy does Jesus use in these verses to describe your relationship with Him?** _____
_____
_____

What is God's desire for your relationship with Jesus? _____
_____
_____

What is "fruit" in this passage of Scripture? _____
_____
_____

What is the evidence you are a disciple of Jesus? _____
_____
_____

Jesus used the analogy of a vine and its branches to describe your relationship with Him. Jesus is the vine. You are a branch. God is the Gardener. Your relationship with Christ is like that of the branch to a vine. Jesus explained that a branch was incapable of producing fruit on its own. Therefore, without Christ, the Vine, you can do nothing.

The "fruit" in this passage is the character of Christ in your life that produces God-like actions toward others. The essential teaching is that the result of Christ's vine-branch relationship with you results in character and behavior that bring glory to God. The fruit of your relationship with Jesus gives evidence that you are His disciple.

What is the source of that fruit—our efforts or Jesus' presence? The source of the Christlike actions in your life is your moment-by-moment relationship with Him, not the good things you do for God. Just as you can know false prophets by what they do, you can tell true disciples of Jesus by how they act in relationship to God and others.

Read *Galatians 5:22-23* on page 125. The fruit of the Spirit is actions that reflect the character of Christ in your life. Living in the Spirit produces character that results in Christlike emotions and habits. You can't set out to be more loving, joyful, and patient by your efforts. These are the result of Christ's living in you and transforming you into His likeness. You will be loving when the Spirit of Christ produces it in your life, not because you decided at the end of a worship service that you needed to be that way toward your family and friends.

So, you may ask, How does God produce this fruit in my life? Do I do anything to encourage these things? Remember that the fruit of the Spirit is not about effort on your part. It is about transformation on God's part. You don't decide to change and take a course in the subject. God transforms you as His relationship with you produces evidence of fruit in your life. You change because of who you are in Christ, not because of what you decide to do. God changes you from your heart to your actions.

There are some things you can do to enhance your relationship with Jesus. Just as the gardener waters, tills, and fertilizes the plants, you can do things to create a healthier environment for Christ to change you into His likeness. Those practices are our topics for the rest of this week.

> *The fruit of the Spirit is love, joy, peace, patience, kindness, goodness, faithfulness, gentleness and self-control. Against such things there is no law (Gal. 5:22-23).*

SUMMARY

- Change is more the result of who you are in Christ, not what you do.
- Conformity to God's image comes as a result of a relationship with Christ, not your effort to be like Him.
- Jesus taught that your actions are the result of who you are.
- The source of the Christlike actions in your life is your moment-by-moment relationship with Jesus, not the good things you do for God.
- Living in the Spirit produces character that results in Christlike emotions and habits.

PERSONAL REFLECTION

Prayerfully complete these activities in your Identity Journal.

1. **At the beginning of today's study, you wrote about a struggle you are experiencing. What have you done to address this issue? Was it effective? Why or why not? Where are you now in the process?**
2. **Write a response to the statement, "Christianity is not a self-help course."**
3. **Explain the difference between change by your efforts and change by God's work in your life. How does that fit with your understanding of what the Bible states about how change happens in a Christian's life? What questions do you have as you seek to change into the likeness of Jesus?**
4. **How did Jesus' analogy of the good tree and bad tree help you understand yourself? How can you apply "you shall know them by their fruit" in your life? How did Jesus' analogy of the vine and the branches help you understand your relationship with Him better?**

DAY 2
IMITATORS OF GOD

"Be imitators of God, therefore, as dearly loved children and live a life of love, just as Christ loved us and gave himself up for us as a fragrant offering and sacrifice to God"
(Eph. 5:1-2).

TODAY YOU WILL ...

❍ recall someone you have imitated in your life;
❍ examine what it means to be an apprentice to Jesus;
❍ examine the biblical call to imitate God as a loved child; and,
❍ write ways you can be like Jesus today.

"Imitation is the highest form of flattery." I don't know who said that, but it's true. We imitate those we respect and like the most. People like to imitate those they consider to be successful or to have some trait they want in their lives. People resist copying those who have things in their lives they don't want. When I was in high school, I wanted to imitate my pastor. He had a doctoral degree, taught at the college level, and even preached from his Greek New Testament. I guess it is no surprise that I have a Ph.D., have taught at the seminary level, and can preach from my Greek New Testament. I imitated my pastor.

I did not intentionally set out to be like that pastor. My parents, however, held him up as someone to be like. My mother took a Greek course he taught at the church. My father served as a deacon with this pastor. Our families were close. It only followed that when I sensed God's call on my life to equip others for ministry, I would model much of how I did things after that man.

Imitation is not just a form of flattery. Imitation is often how you acquire skills and direction in life. You imitate those you think are important or who have something in their lives you want for your own.

This imitation may be intentional or unintentional, but you become whom you want to be like. It follows, then, that you need to pay close attention to whom you imitate.

✚ **You may have had someone in your life you imitated. Who is that person, and what have you imitated? If you compared your lives, what would be the same? What would be different? Write your thoughts and be prepared to share them in your Identity Group.**

Imitation Is a Form of Discipleship

As we mentioned earlier in this study, being a disciple is being a learner. Disciples learn a way of life or lesson about life from their teacher. To be a disciple of another is to imitate the teacher. Discipleship is a form of imitation. When you say you are a disciple or follower of Jesus you are saying, *I am learning a way of life from Jesus.* Others should see evidence of the ways you have modeled your life after Him.

I like Dallas Willard's extended definition of a disciple. He wrote, "a disciple, or apprentice, is simply someone who has decided to be with another person, under appropriate conditions, in order to become capable of doing what that person does or to become what that person is."[1] Willard calls being a disciple of Jesus being an apprentice to Jesus. This image describes what you are to do as a follower of Jesus: you are to become capable of doing what Jesus did or become who Jesus is.

An apprentice to Jesus is different from someone who studies about Jesus. When Jesus called you to follow Him, He intended that you become like Him. He expected you to change from what you were to who He is. That change will not come by effort alone, but when you make yourself His apprentice, you will spend much effort to conform your ways to His ways. "We are changed by Jesus not because we observe him but because we dare to follow him."[2] Answering Jesus' call to follow Him is to answer His call to become a learner.

How do you apprentice yourself to Jesus? First, remember that He chose you. You did not choose Him. (See *John 15:16.*) That means you don't set the agenda. The Master Teacher decides what the apprentice should and can do. Second, to follow Jesus is to obey Him. You demonstrate your love for Jesus as you do what He says. He said, " *'If you love me, you will obey what I command' " (John 14:15).* Apprentices learn their trade by obeying their master's commandments in the studio or workshop. Disciples learn their trade by obeying the Master's commands in the kitchen or community.

✚ **Record your thoughts about being an apprentice to Jesus in your Identity Journal. Consider a skill or characteristic Jesus demonstrated that you desire to have in your own life. List ways you can literally follow Jesus in order to acquire that skill or characteristic. Put the ideas you have listed into action.**

Imitate God

One of Jesus' many followers who became like Him was Paul. Paul was a person who understood what being an apprentice meant, and he called others to become followers of Jesus. Let's look at an example from the life of Paul.

Be imitators of God, therefore, as dearly loved children and live a life of love, just as Christ loved us and gave himself up for us as a fragrant offering and sacrifice to God (Eph. 5:1-2).

Read Ephesians 5:1-2. Who did Paul call the Ephesians to imitate? _____

Do you consider his instructions even a possibility?
○ **Yes**   ○ **No**   ○ **Maybe**

How is it possible to imitate God? _____
_____
_____

What did Paul ask them to do as they imitated God? _____
_____
_____

Whose example were they to follow while living that way? _____
_____
_____

Paul called the Christians in Ephesus to "imitate God." That's right, imitate God. We get our English word *mimic* from the transliterated Greek word translated *imitate.* Mimic is much more than "monkey see, monkey do." It means to fold into your life the habits and attitudes of the one you imitate. What is the basis of such a seemingly outlandish demand? Paul said to do this *as dearly loved children.* Now do you see? Your identity is a child of God. As a loved child, you want to be like the One who loves you and provides for you. So, you seek to imitate those things about that One you love so deeply. It is no different from a child wanting to be like a loving parent. God loves you, and you want to be like your Father in heaven.

You may ask, *What can I imitate about God?* Please! It's God you're talking about here! Paul wrote that you mimic God like a loved child imitates the love of his or her parents. If a parent models love for a child, he or she will show that same love to others. The opposite is also true. Therefore, you mimic God by living a life of love like Him. *Live* in this verse can be literally translated *walk.* It can also mean a way of life or lifestyle. Paul wrote that you imitate God by making His love the way you live your life. Others should see evidences of God's love in your choices and how you treat others.

Guiding Others

The highest goal of an apprentice is to become a master tradesman who can take on apprentices of his own. At our church, our goal is to make disciples who make disciples. Jesus expects you to become a master tradesman so you can enlist your own apprentices to His ways. That is what Jesus meant when He commissioned His disciples to make disciples of all ethnic groups. (Read *Matt. 28:19-20*.) Jesus commissioned His apprentices to become master disciples in order to enlist and train others who have submitted themselves to the call of Jesus on their lives.

Paul understood this principle when he wrote to the Corinthian Christians, *Imitate me (1 Cor. 4:16)*. He also told them to *Follow my example, as I follow the example of Christ (1 Cor. 11:1)*. In both places, he used the same word from which we get our English word *mimic*. He essentially said, Mimic me as I mimic Jesus. Paul, a master disciple, invited his apprentices to follow him so they could learn what he learned from Jesus.

Jesus called you to do the same when you accepted His call on your life. You are to become like Jesus while leading and teaching others to live His lifestyle and know His ways. Other followers of Jesus are part of the fruit your life in Christ can be yielding.

> *"Therefore go and make disciples of all nations, baptizing them in the name of the Father and of the Son and of the Holy Spirit, and teaching them to obey everything I have commanded you. And surely I am with you always, to the very end of the age"* (Matt. 28:19-20).

✚ **Make a list of five ways you can imitate Jesus today. Consider who you will see and what you will do. The time-honored question, "What would Jesus do?" is appropriate. Return to the list at the end of the day and check the items you did. If you did not do some of them, write reasons why. Be prepared to share your list and results with your Identity Group.**

○ **1.** _____
○ **2.** _____
○ **3.** _____
○ **4.** _____
○ **5.** _____

SUMMARY

- You imitate those you think are important or who have something in their lives you want for your own.
- A disciple is an apprentice to another to learn what that person does or become like that person.
- When Jesus called you to follow Him, He intended that you change from what you were to who He is.
- Paul wrote that you imitate God by living a life of love like Him.
- Jesus expects you to become a master tradesman in His way of life so you can enlist your own apprentices to His ways.

PERSONAL REFLECTION

⊕ **Prayerfully complete these activities in your Identity Journal.**

1. **What are some negative implications of imitating others? What are some improper motivations for being like others?**
2. **A disciple is an apprentice. Would you consider yourself a disciple of Jesus? Which of His skills and habits have you adopted?**
3. **Imitating God's love is quite a high order. What are some actions you can take to imitate Jesus' sacrificial love toward you to others? List people who are closest to you. Then write one way you can love each one like Jesus loves them.**
4. **Jesus desires you to become a master teacher so you can make other disciples. Evaluate yourself as an apprentice to Jesus. Could anyone recognize that you are ready to train others to follow Jesus? If not, what areas do you need to improve?**

[1]Dallas Willard, *The Divine Conspiracy* (San Francisco: HarperCollins, 1998), 282.
[2]From *Jesus on Leadership* by C. Gene Wilkes © 1999 LifeWay Press. Used by permission of Tyndale House Publishers, Inc. All rights reserved.

DAY 3

HABITS THAT TRANSFORM, PART 1

"Being confident of this, that he who began a good work in you will carry it on to completion until the day of Christ Jesus"
(Phil. 1:6).

TODAY YOU WILL ...

○ recall an experience in which you learned the value of practice and/ or good habits;
○ examine the biblical metaphors of farming and being an athlete as ways to grow into the likeness of Jesus;
○ define a "spiritual discipline"; and,
○ examine habits in Jesus' life that you can practice in your life.

My youngest daughter made the school basketball team her seventh grade year. Like any sport, basketball demands discipline. Repetition is the key to learning, and in basketball you do many repetitions. Drills, they call them. They do dribbling drills. They practice lay ups, jump shots, and free throws. Over and over, again and again. She often would come home and answer my question, "How was practice?" with "I wish we would play sometimes. All we do is practice." I would try to say something encouraging like, "Practice makes perfect" or "Someday all that work will pay off." I knew how boring practice could be if you were not as talented or as sold-out as others on the team.

One day all that practice did pay off. It was late in the game, and my daughter was fouled while shooting. That meant two free throws since she missed the shot. Both teams lined up. The opposing team on the bench began to chant "Miss it. Miss it." She shot and made the first one! Applause and cheers. The opposing crowd yelled louder. Mom and Dad cheered even louder. The referee handed her the ball again. She stepped to the line, went through her routine, shot, and made the second one! You would have thought she had won the game. (They were behind 15 points.) But, two consecutive free throws for a seventh-grader on the school's B Team were a big deal. You know what? She continued to practice after that. Funny how practice takes on a different meaning when you experience a little success.

⊕ **Did you play a sport or musical instrument in school? Be prepared to share your most successful moment with your Identity Group at your next meeting. Also, share what you learned through participating in that sport or playing that instrument about the value of practice or developing habits.**

Farmer or Athlete?

Growing in the likeness of Christ is like the growth of a plant or the training of an athlete. Both pictures are in the Bible. Jesus called you to stay in a vine/branch relationship with Him. If you do, He promised you would experience the power of His presence in your life. You will bear evidence of His Spirit *(John 15:1-8)*. Your part is to remain in relationship with the Vine. You can also till, water, and fertilize the soil of your life. The vine and branch will grow as the ground provides for growth and as you stay in relationship with the Vine.

Paul, in contrast, described his walk with the Lord in athletic terms. He told of beating his body into submission so he would not be disqualified from the race *(1 Cor. 9:27)*. He talked of pressing forward to win the prize of his high calling *(Phil. 3:14)*. The implication is that you train to prepare for God to work in your life. You vigorously prepare your body, mind, and soul for the race of becoming like Jesus.

So, which way of life should you adopt? Should you be a gardener or an athlete in your relationship with Christ? The answer is, you pick. One emphasizes God growing in your life while you stay in relationship with Jesus and work to keep the soil in optimum condition for growth. The other stresses training yourself to allow God to work through your life. Both include the life force of God's presence and your efforts to allow God's love to grow.

Becoming like Jesus is a balance between allowing God to change you and intentionally making changes in your life. The key word is *balance*. You live out your identity in Christ by letting God complete the good work He started in you, while disciplining your natural self to allow God to work more freely in your life. You did nothing but accept God's offer to become His adopted child. Now that you are His child, you want to do whatever you can in response to His love for you to enhance your relationship with Him. Your walk with the Lord is that love response to God.

Practice that Counts

The purpose of practice is to develop habits that enhance your performance. Concert pianists practice scales hours a day so that when they perform before thousands, their fingers hit each note as it was composed. Professional golfers hit hundreds of balls before and after a round so that when they are on the course they can choose from a bag of shots. They develop habits on the driving range and chipping and putting greens that allow them to make tournament-winning shots on the course. Practice develops habits that lead to successful performance.

This truth applies to your transformation into the likeness of Jesus. If you have accepted God's call to be an apprentice to Jesus, then practicing His lifestyle will develop habits that allow you to perform successfully in the game of life. In church life, these habits are called *spiritual disciplines.* They are habits you develop in your life that allow God to change you into the likeness of His Son.

Doug Rumford, a pastor in Fresno, California, recalls a ski instructor telling him that a muscle needs to repeat an action about two hundred times to remember what it is supposed to do. The idea of practice, the instructor said, is to build muscle memory. He remembered her saying, "Do it right, again and again, and your muscles will gain the habit you want. You'll begin to react without effort, without even thinking."[1] Doug applied this to the practice of spiritual discipline. He wrote, "Spiritual discipline, then, is developing soul reflexes so that we know how to live. We discipline ourselves to develop soul memory in normal times so that we'll be equipped for the times of high demand or deep crisis."[2]

"Soul reflexes" and "soul memory" are refreshing concepts to describe the goal of spiritual disciplines. They describe the results of practicing the habits of Jesus. The other thing Doug's insights teach is that you don't practice in crisis. You practice "in normal times" so you will be prepared when the bases are loaded with two outs in the bottom of the ninth and you are behind, or, when you are tempted to sin against God.

Habits of Jesus

Since Jesus is your master tradesman who has called you to follow Him and make others followers, too, let's look at some of His habits and seek ways to practice them in your life.

⊕ **Read the following passages in your Bible and record the habit observed in Jesus' life.**

Luke 6:12 _____

Luke 7:36 _____

Luke 9:28 _____

Luke 13:10 _____

133

Some of Jesus' habits were that He prayed often and sometimes all night *(Luke 6:12)*. He willingly accepted invitations from those He sought to reach *(Luke 7:36)*. He often took others with Him to quiet places to pray *(Luke 9:28)*. Jesus assembled with God's people on the Sabbath and taught others about God *(Luke 13:10)*. These are just some of Jesus' habits, things He did repeatedly, that are recorded in the Gospels. You may want to choose one of the Gospels and read through it to mark things Jesus did regularly. Consider how you can incorporate them in your life.

Jesus' habits are transferable to your life. When Jesus said, *"Follow me,"* He meant it literally. Jesus expected His followers to imitate His habits in their lives.

⊕ **List habits Jesus practiced in His life. Then personalize each one to your life by listing ways you can develop the same habits. (For example, Jesus prayed often. You can practice prayer by setting aside time each day to talk with God. Over time, prayer can become a daily habit that allows you to have an ongoing relationship with God.) You may want to record these in your Identity Journal so you can keep track of how you are progressing.**

Jesus' Habit	My Practice
_____	_____
_____	_____
_____	_____
_____	_____

A Word of Caution

Spiritual disciplines exist to help you become more like Jesus. They are exercises that allow your spirit to grow. But they can also consume your attention to the point that your goal becomes doing the habit, not allowing God to transform you. Remember that your status and standing before God in Christ will not change if you do not develop spiritual habits in your life. Your relationship with God does not depend on your efforts. Only His grace counts. (See *Titus 3:4-7.*) On the other hand, just like neglecting a loved one results in a disintegration of the relationship, so neglecting your relationship with God by not participating in your transformation will prevent your experiencing the fullness of God.

Following Jesus means developing habits that help you be like Him.

SUMMARY

- Growing in the likeness of Christ is like the growth of a plant and the training of an athlete.
- Becoming like Jesus is a balance between allowing God to change you and intentionally making changes yourself.

• Spiritual disciplines are habits you develop that allow God to change you into the likeness of His Son.
• Jesus' habits are transferable to your life. When Jesus said, "Follow me," He meant it literally. Jesus expected His followers to imitate His habits.

PERSONAL REFLECTION

✠ **Prayerfully complete these activities in your Identity Journal.**

1. **Do you consider yourself a disciplined person? What are some habits you have intentionally developed?**
2. **Is this the first time you have considered developing habits in your spiritual life? Make a list of reasons why you feel spiritual habits can or cannot help you live as a person in Christ.**
3. **Since you are an apprentice to Jesus, which of the habits you studied today will you begin to develop first? What plan have you written down to help you develop that habit?**
4. **Write several other easily-attainable goals related to deepening your walk with the Lord.**

---

[1]*SoulShaping* by Dr. Douglas J. Rumford © 1996. Used by permission of Tyndale House Publishers, Inc. All rights reserved.
[2]Ibid., 87.

DAY 4

HABITS THAT TRANSFORM, PART 2

"Therefore, my dear friends, as you have always obeyed—not only in my presence, but now much more in my absence—continue to work out your salvation with fear and trembling, for it is God who works in you to will and to act according to his good purpose" (Phil. 2:12-13).

TODAY YOU WILL ...

❍ recall an individual who modeled the truth that practice enhances performance;
❍ examine the concept of "spiritual workout";
❍ discover the source of energy for spiritual practice; and,
❍ commit your lifestyle to the glory of God.

Kurt Warner should not have been in the Super Bowl. If you had told anyone four years earlier he would be named the NFL's Most Valuable Player, the Super Bowl's Most Valuable Player, and would be the quarterback of the Super Bowl champions St. Louis Rams, they would have laughed. The experts said he couldn't play in the NFL or the Canadian Football league team. He finally landed a quarterback job with an Arena Football league after being passed over by the NFL draft year after year. In 1998, the St. Louis Rams signed him, and he played only one game that year. The following year he stayed with the team because no one else wanted him. When the highly paid starting quarterback was injured, Kurt stepped in and led the team to a Super Bowl victory! He never stopped practicing. He never gave up on his dream—even when he was stocking groceries at the Hy-Vee supermarket in Cedar Falls, Iowa.

Who does Kurt Warner give the credit for his rise to celebrity status? He does not credit his hard work or his persistence. Kurt Warner gives credit to Jesus Christ. You see, four years before his rise to football glory, Kurt gave his life to Christ. His then girlfriend, Brenda, led him to the Lord as he watched her respond in faith to the tragic deaths of her parents. After trusting Christ and being baptized, he married Brenda and adopted her daughter and son. He attends church with his family and Rams receiver, Isaac Bruce.

Kurt Warner is open about his faith in Christ. From his "First Things First" foundation Web site you can read his confession:

> ... I realize my role here on earth is not to throw touchdown passes and win football games, although that is the position and the platform that I have been given. I realize my goal is to win as many people to Jesus as possible.[1]

⊕ **Think of someone you admire because he or she has excelled in an area that interests you. What do you know about his or her faith? What about his or her practice habits? How does practice affect performance? Which habits of this person can you apply to your life? Write your thoughts and be prepared to share them in your Identity Group.**

Work Out!

Practice alone did not make Kurt Warner a world champion. He had God-given talent and athletic abilities that few people have. Through practice he honed his talents. He was a good steward of the gift God gave him even when he was not in the league he wanted to play in. I could practice as many hours as Warner has, but since my gift is different, I could never reach the heights he reached. The talent was Warner's. Practice enhanced his gift and prepared him to excel when the opportunity offered itself.

Spiritual disciplines are like practice. They do not create the gift. They enhance the gift God has given you through His grace. Any effort on your part allows God's Spirit more freedom to grow and influence your transformation into His likeness. You do not practice to create the gift. You practice to develop the gift and to be prepared when God gives you an opportunity to act or speak for Him. Practice also prepares you for spiritual warfare when the Evil One ambushes you.

The apostle Paul loved his friends in Philippi. He filled his letter with encouragement and kindness. Early in the letter, he explained how he wanted them to continue in the work God began in their lives.

⊕ **Read Philippians 2:12-13. What did Paul say to his friends?**

_____

_____

> *Therefore, my dear friends, as you have always obeyed—not only in my presence, but now much more in my absence—continue to work out your salvation with fear and trembling (Phil. 2:12-13).*

Paul had asked the Philippians to have the same attitude as Jesus *(Phil. 2:5)*. He then described Jesus' example which they were to follow *(Phil. 2:6-11)*. They were to conform their attitudes to Jesus' example. How were they supposed to do that?

Paul acknowledged that his friends always did what he told them to do *(Phil. 2:12)*. Paul was their master tradesman in how to follow Jesus, and they followed his directions. Notice, too, that he said they did so even when he was not with them. Maturity is practicing without the coach or teacher looking over your shoulder. Also, good coaches always find something to encourage in their players.

Paul then told them to continue to *work out* their salvation *with fear and trembling (Phil. 2:12)*. He is not telling them to work out their salvation because they should be afraid of their time before God at judgment day. You can do nothing to secure your relationship with God but to trust Jesus. So, what was Paul telling them to do?

The word for *work out* and the adjective for salvation are plural. Paul was addressing the entire church, not an individual. The church with its many members was to bring to completion the salvation God had given to them. That salvation was to show up in their daily lives. Paul was specific about what that looked like in *Philippians 2:14-18*. All of this was to be done trusting that God would complete this "good work" that He had begun among them *(Phil. 1:6)*.

By referring to fear and trembling Paul told his readers to exercise daily the salvation that God had given them. They were to experience the same attitude Jesus exemplified when He came to do the Father's will for His life. They also were to respect and honor others as they lived like Jesus.

✦ **How can Paul's words apply to you as you are transformed into the likeness of Jesus? Read Philippians 2:1-5 and Philippians 2:14-16 in your Bible. List attitudes and actions that are in your life if you are "working out" God's gift of salvation. For example, Paul says, "Do everything without complaining or arguing."**

_____

_____

_____

_____

_____

_____

_____

_____

_____

This list of attitudes and actions is like the fruit we learned about yesterday. In your vine/branch relationship with Jesus, He is transforming you into His likeness. Paul's list of instructions flows not from your efforts to be better, but from Christ's influence on your character and behavior. Your private spiritual practice results in public displays of Christ's character in your life.

Energy Booster

Have you ever run out of energy? When I went to a gym with a friend I could not get over the number of energy-boosting products sold there—until I ran out of energy! Then, I was pleased they had many to choose from! Energy is essential to working out. You cannot continue without it. Where do you get spiritual energy so you can *work out* God's gift of salvation in your life and the life of the church?

Philippians 2:13 begins, *"for it is God who works in you to will and to act."* The word for *work* here is different from the words *to work out* in the previous verse. We get our English word *energy* from this transliterated Greek word. Eugene Peterson paraphrases the verse this way, *"That energy is God's energy, an energy deep within you, God himself willing and working at what will give him the most pleasure" (The Message).*[2] God is the energy you need to work out the implications of His salvation in your life. His Holy Spirit energizes you to accomplish all He desires for you. You exercise. God provides the energy.

Spiritual Workouts

Spiritual habits, or disciplines, are what you practice on your own so you can perform as Christ. You develop these spiritual habits through daily practice so you can respond like Jesus in any given situation. You cannot walk into the Super Bowl and expect to win if you have never played before! How can so many Christians think they can overcome temptation when they have never read their Bible or prayed? How can you defeat an enemy you have never read anything about? How can you respond to the needs of others if you have never known the depth of God's love in Jesus?

It is beyond the scope of this study to provide a manual of "workouts" to enhance the gift of salvation God has placed in your life. I do, however, want to introduce you to some workouts that can allow God to transform you into the likeness of Jesus.[3] With Bible study, prayer, and worship come service to others; fasting from food, media, and physical stimuli; study to enhance your understanding of the Bible; stewardship of time, talent and treasures; and simplicity of lifestyle.

⊕ **What other habits can you identify that God can use to transform you into His likeness? Be prepared to share them with your Identity Group at your next meeting.**

Practice for the Love of Him

Practice of any discipline takes commitment. Beyond commitment, practice comes from a love for what you are seeking to develop or who you are trying to become. Your motivation to practice spiritual habits in your life should not be personal commitment alone. Your motivation to practice the habits of Jesus comes from your love and desire to become like the One who gave His life for you. Commitment will follow this love. If you love Him, you will obey Him. And, if you obey Him, you will make time to work out His gift of salvation.

✤ **Close today's study with a quiet time of expressing your love for God and your willingness to practice His habits so He can work in you to will and to act according to his good purpose (Phil. 2:13). Acknowledge His transforming power in your life.**

SUMMARY

• Spiritual disciplines are like practice. They do not create the gift, they enhance the gift God has given you through His grace.
• Paul instructed the church to bring to completion the salvation God had given them. That salvation was to show up in their daily lives.
• God is the energy you need to practice or work out the implications of God's salvation in your daily life.
• You develop spiritual habits through daily practice so you can respond like Jesus in any given situation.
• Your motivation to practice the habits of Jesus comes from your love and desire to become like the One who gave His life for you.

PERSONAL REFLECTION

✤ **Prayerfully complete these activities in your Identity Journal.**

1. **What skill or discipline have you spent time developing in your life? How good are you at it? How much time do you spend developing this skill or discipline?**
2. **What are some implications from Paul's letter to the Philippians for your life? Apply the concept of God being your "energy" for practice to your daily life.**
3. **The practice of spiritual habits prepares you to live like Jesus. What spiritual habits have you developed that have helped you succeed according to his good purpose? What new habits can you develop?**
4. **Is your love for Jesus truly your motivation to practice His habits?**

---

[1]Kurt Warner First Things First Foundation: Kurt's Testimonial [online], [cited 27 May 2005]. Available from Internet: *www.firstthingsfirstfoundation.com/testimonials_kurt..html*
[2]Scriptures marked The Message are from The Message. Copyright © by Eugene H. Peterson 1993, 1994, 1995, 1996, 2000, 2001, 2202. Used by permission of NavPress Publishing Group.
[3]Some books that may be helpful are *Soulshaping* by Dr. Douglas J. Rumford, © 1996. Used by permission of Tyndale House Publishers, Inc. All rights reserved; Dallas Willard, *The Divine Conspiracy: Rediscovering Our Hidden Life in God* (San Francisco: HarperCollins, 1998) and *The Spirit of the Disciplines: Understanding How God Changes Lives* (San Francisco: HarperCollins, 1990); and Richard J. Foster, *Celebration of Discipline: The Path to Spiritual Growth* (San Francisco: HarperCollins, 1988).

DAY 5

NOW, LIVE LIKE IT!

Only let us live up to what we have already attained (Phil. 3:16).

TODAY YOU WILL ...

○ recall a time you overcame adversity and what kept you going;
○ examine Paul's instructions on how to continue to live out your identity in Christ;
○ examine Paul's encouragement to the Philippians to "press on" to those things Christ has attained for them; and,
○ be encouraged to commit to a lifelong pursuit of living out your identity in Christ.

Michelle Akers played on the US Women's Soccer team that won the World Cup in 1999. If you remember, Brandi Chastain decided the game on a final goal kick after a tied game in regulation. Where was Michelle during the last tense moments of the match against China? She was in the locker room trying to get enough energy from IVs to get back on the field. Michelle suffers from Chronic Fatigue Syndrome—not an illness any world-class athlete would want. Not only that, five years earlier she lay on her bed and could not get up. She was diagnosed with Chronic Fatigue *and* Immune Dysfunction Syndrome. Her marriage had ended and her soccer career looked like it was over. Her high school soccer coach had led her to trust Christ, but she tried to go to church on Sunday but however she wanted the rest of the week. When her life crashed around her, she finally gave everything to Christ. Michelle wrote in her journal:

> But as I look back at how far I've come, I realize God has blessed me. And is still blessing me. ... So through these hard times—CFIDS, injuries, divorce—God has forced me to open my eyes, examine my life, and find the "narrow road" again. To listen, love and follow Him. And to trust.[1]

> *Not that I have already obtained all this, or have already been made perfect, but I press on to take hold of that for which Christ Jesus took hold of me. Brothers, I do not consider myself yet to have taken hold of it. But one thing I do: Forgetting what is behind and straining toward what is ahead, I press on toward the goal to win the prize for which God has called me heavenward in Christ Jesus.*
>
> *All of us who are mature should take such a view of things. And if on some point you think differently, that too God will make clear to you. Only let us live up to what we have already attained (Phil. 3:12-16).*

From that experience, Michelle began to grow in the Lord and deal with her weaknesses. The rest of the story is a woman who played 'till she dropped on the field before 90,000 plus fans and shared in the glory of being a world champion.

Just before the 1999 World Cup win over China, she wrote:

> I also know that God has prepared me with perfect precision for this exact moment of challenge and adversity ... I can get knocked down time and time again and still have the strength and desire to get up. And the even cooler then is if I am living out God's will for my life and get totally slammed and my body is totally thrashed ... even though I might not be getting up on the outside, I am still standing up in triumph on the inside.[2]

⊕ **You may have worked through a time of adversity in your life, or you may be working through such a time now. At your next meeting, share your experience with your Identity Group. Tell what thoughts that went through your mind when you were faced with that adversity. Tell what you did or are doing to live it. Share your sources of strength and inspiration.**

"But One Thing I Do"

Your spiritual transformation is a lifelong growing experience. While your identity, status, and standing before God are changed in a moment of trust in Christ Jesus, who you are in that new relationship is realized throughout the rest of your life. Like a child growing into adulthood, you will increasingly grow into the likeness of Jesus. And, in the same way, you will face setbacks and discouragement as long as you remain in this human state.

Paul, the apostle, knew about being an adopted child of God, yet he still faced adversity and trials. He also had a perspective on life that allowed him to press through these challenges and seek to attain what God wanted him to be.

⊕ **Read Philippians 3:12-16. Did Paul assume that he had obtained everything he had prayed for the Philippians?** ○ yes ○ no

What did Paul say he was pressing on to take hold of? _____
_____
_____

Who should have such a view of things? _____
_____
_____

Paul wanted *to know Christ and the power of his resurrection and the fellowship of sharing in his sufferings, becoming like him in his death, and so, somehow, to attain to the resurrection from the dead (Phil. 3:10-11).*

While that was his desire for the Philippians as well, he humbly admitted that he had not obtained those things himself. However, he did "press on" to experience two things. One he mentioned in *verse 12, that for which Christ Jesus took hold of me.* Paul acknowledged that his desire was to press on to experience that which Christ had already secured for him. This is a reference to his salvation and position in Christ. Paul did not secure those things. Christ did. His desire was to experience the implications of what Christ did for him.

He said, *One thing I do.* Paul wrote that his single focus was to press on to *win the prize for which God has called me heavenward in Christ Jesus.* Nothing else mattered. Paul's emphasis was on God's call on his life. He lived to complete what God called him to do, not what he envisioned for his life. Paul had forgotten his past and was moving toward the goal, just like a World Cup soccer player, to experience what God had begun to do in his life. He wanted nothing else.

Mature people, Paul said, live their lives with a focus on Jesus Christ. Maturity means pressing on through life's heartaches and hurts to become what God has already made you in Christ Jesus. Paul concluded, *"Only let us live up to what we have already attained."* He invited his Christian brothers and sisters in Philippi to live up to what they had already attained in their relationship with Jesus. His life was to pursue what Christ had secured for him and to live out God's call on his life. That is all he asked his friends to do. That is what God desires.

"All of Us Who Are Mature"

Based on Paul's words to the Philippians, the goal of the Christian life is to live up to what you have already attained in faith through your relationship with Christ. This is the goal of spiritual transformation.

Your identity, status, and standing "in Christ" are established for you. God did that for you. Who you are in Christ is now the foundation for your decisions and efforts in life. Like Paul, your single focus should be to pursue with all your being who you already are in Christ. All you "do" is allow the presence of God in your life to change your character, which will change your behavior. Maturity in spiritual transformation is realizing God's work is complete for you, and your joyful pursuit is to allow God's work to be complete in and through you.

You are an adopted child of God. You have new spiritual DNA through a new birth. You stand justified, redeemed, and made holy before God. You will be in eternity a coheir with Christ. Live like it! You do not have to become an adopted child of God—you are one in your relationship with Christ! And, because that is your identity in Christ, how you live should reflect that truth!

Flip through this workbook. Record in the margin one or two primary teachings that sum up this study for you. What helped you most?

1. _____

2. _____

✣ **Complete the following as an act of commitment to live up to what you have already attained in your relationship with Christ. Be prepared to share your completed sentence with your Identity Group.**

My identity in Christ is _____,
therefore, I commit to live my life to _____.

What Next?

Your next step in this journey of spiritual transformation is to keep the truths of God's Word about who you are in Christ in your heart and mind. As you make your relationship with Christ the "one thing" in your life, God promises to change you into the likeness of Jesus.

First, continue recording your relationship with Christ in your Identity Journal. This will be a great source of strength and encouragement as you mature in Christ. And, second become part of and serve with a group of God's adopted children. The Bible calls it the church. Hopefully, you have experienced some of God's intention for the church through your Identity Group, but you need to network with others who are becoming like Jesus and who are on mission to make disciples. Few things will help you more in this transformation process than to be part of the body of Christ.

SUMMARY

- While your identity, status, and standing before God are changed in a moment of trust in Christ Jesus, who you are in that new relationship is realized throughout the rest of your life.
- Maturity means pressing on through life's heartaches and hurts to become what God has already made you in Christ Jesus.
- The goal of spiritual transformation is to live out what is already complete in your relationship with Christ.
- You are an adopted child of God. You have new spiritual DNA as a result of your new birth. You stand justified, redeemed, and made holy before God. And you will be in eternity as a coheir with Jesus Christ. Live like it!

PERSONAL REFLECTION

✣ **Prayerfully complete these activities in your Identity Journal.**

1. **What were your feelings about Michelle Aker's ordeal? What is your reaction to her greatest sports moment?**
2. **Pursuing a goal like a hunter sounds like a lot of effort. Write some practical things you can do to pursue knowing Christ as**

God desires you to know Him. What implications do these things have for how you live your life?

3. What are signs of maturity in a person's life? How do you know when you are mature rather than just older? How can you apply Paul's teachings about spiritual maturity in your life?

4. List ways you can "live up to what we have already attained" in Christ. This can include attitudes and habits that should be present in the life of a person who lives like they know who they are in Christ.

---

[1]Michelle Akers, *The Game and the Glory* (Grand Rapids, MI: Zondervan Publishing House, 2000), 180, 228.
[2]Ibid.

GUIDELINES FOR LEADING IDENTITY GROUPS

The following information is for the facilitator of a *My Identity in Christ* Identity Group. Each week this section will guide your group to spend sharing time together. Adapt suggestions to meet the needs and goals of the group. Included are answers to a few questions and guidelines for seven one-hour Identity Group sessions. Don't let this guide restrict your sharing. Freely follow the Holy Spirit's leadership.

What Is the Goal of My Identity in Christ?

The goal is not to finish another workbook and have more knowledge about God. The goal is to provide biblical principles that can aid each student to know who he or she is in Christ and how to live daily like Christ. Think of this study more as a manual for living than as a workbook filled with information.

How Can This Material Be Used?

You can use this study several ways. Any student can use the workbook for individual study. You can also make it part of an ongoing discipleship ministry You can use it as part of your cell-group or small-group ministry. It can also be incorporated into a mentoring relationship with a new or growing Christian.

Who Participates in This Study?

This study is for maturing Christian students. This includes new Christians or those who first trusted Christ some time ago. Both are seeking to grow in their relationship with God through Jesus Christ. The study helps Christian students know who they are in Christ and that God can transform them into the likeness of Jesus. It is based on spiritual transformation: God's work of changing a believer into the likeness of Jesus by creating a new identity in Christ and by empowering a lifelong relationship of love, trust, and obedience to glorify God.

When and How Often Do Groups Meet?

My Identity in Christ is a six-week study. Each week's study covers one topic in five daily lessons. Review the Contents (p. 3) for the topics and progression of the study. Students will need 30 to 45 minutes to complete each daily study. Time will vary according to each participant's desire and ability to complete the work.

Your Identity Group will meet seven times. The goal of the first meeting is to introduce participants to one another and to the study. At this time you will distribute workbooks. Meeting seven consecutive weeks maintains continuity. Plan a minimum of an hour for each Identity Group meeting. If you meet in a home and provide snacks and/or a time of worship, plan for an hour and a half to two hours.

Where Should Groups Meet?

You can meet at the church or in a school or home. Choose a place that best suits the needs of the group and your goals for offering this study. Advise participants prior to the first session where you will meet. At the first meeting you can decide if that is the best place for the group. You may want to rotate locations.

What Is an Identity Group, Identity Partner, and Identity Journal?

The **Identity Group** is essential to experiencing the full intent of the material. It is a group of eight to ten people who are doing the study together. The group can be larger or smaller, but the larger the group, the less the interaction. The group provides support and encouragement for each member. Members also provide prayer support for each other. Participants will be asked to share answers and insights from their study with this group at each meeting. This interaction will be the heart of the weekly Identity Group meetings. As facilitator, always be prepared to minister to the needs of any participant during the group meetings. The information shared may become emotional and self-revealing, so be sensitive to needs in the group each week.

Each participant chooses another person in the Identity Group to be his or her partner during the duration of the study. These **Identity Partners** will be encouragers during the study. Identity Partners will talk with each other between group meetings. Partners are prayer partners and confidants for each other. An ideal relationship would be for one partner to be a more mature Christian who can encourage the other to become more like Jesus as they go through the study.

The **Identity Journal** is an effective way for participants to record what God reveals to them beyond the contents of the workbook. Encourage students to purchase a binder or spiral notebook for their journal. Suggestions at the end of each day's study lead participants to make entries in their journals.

What Does the Facilitator Need?

You are the facilitator of this study, most likely, because someone asked you to do it. You don't have to know all the biblical passages and principles in this workbook before facilitating the group. Do complete each week's study before leading a group. Follow the instructions in this group plan. It will guide you to answers to questions and provide comments to make. Students will provide answers and insights from their personal studies during the week. Each participant will need a Bible (NIV is the primary text used for the study) and a workbook. Encourage the use of the Identity Journal. Worksheets for group sessions are provided following this section.

You will need an open and compassionate heart. Each participant will come at his or her own level of maturity in a relationship with Christ. Do not expect everyone to progress at the same speed. Do not be judgmental of those who may lag behind or not understand the information. You are a mentor to the group, not the answer person. Plan to spend extra time outside the group meetings to nurture those who may need you. Your purpose as the facilitator is to help people know and live their identity in Christ.

Given the fact that every student has these guidelines for leading Identity Groups in her workbook, feel free to ask mature students to facilitate a session or two. This will help develop leaders in your group.

What Does a Typical Meeting Look Like?

While each meeting should be customized to fit the needs and goals of your group, a typical meeting might follow this format:

- Opening Prayer Time (5 min.)
- Group Interaction Activity (5 min.)
- Group Sharing (40 min.)
- Review This Week's Assignments (5 min.)
- Closing Prayer Time (5 min.)

The majority of the time will be spent answering questions from the previous week's study. It is not necessary to answer every question listed in the Group Sharing time. Choose those that fit the needs of your students best. Remember, the goal is not to get all the answers right but to lead students to a deeper understanding of who they are in Christ and how to live like Him. Participation in the sharing time is for personal growth not for making grades.

How Are Participants Enlisted?

Students live busy lives. Most are not looking for something else to do. Use youth group publications, announcement times, Christian radio stations, and other means to promote the study. Most churches need four to six weeks of publicity prior to the first meeting for members to know about a study. Another way to encourage students to enroll is to have someone give a testimony in a weekly meeting as to what the study has done to help that person understand his or her identity in Christ or deal with identity issues as a student. At the end of the service, provide a sign-up sheet for students to enroll.

SESSION 1

Goal: To introduce students to one another and to the study.

Opening Prayer (5 min.)

Pray that each member will encounter Christ in a new and meaningful way. Pray that they will recognize their identity in Christ and desire to grow in His likeness.

Group Interaction Activity (5 min.)

Instruct participants to take their wallets or purses and find four items that identify them. This may include a driver's license, membership cards, picture of family members, or receipts. Have members display each item and explain how it identifies them. Allow time for everyone in the group to share. Begin by sharing your items. When you finish say: **We will spend the next seven weeks discovering our identity, but not by examining things that we just looked at. We will spend our time examining God's Word and seeing that our identity is in Christ.**

Group Sharing (40 min.)

1. Distribute workbooks. Review the Introduction on page 5 together. Ask, **What are the two reasons given as to why this is such an important study?**

2. Ask participants to share their stories about their families of origin. This will help everyone know the members of the group and prepare them to answer questions in the first week of study.

3. Share that this study is about how God can transform your identity from whoever you are in earthly terms to who you are "in Christ Jesus." Emphasize that these lessons will lead each of you to God's Word to discover your identity in Christ Jesus, your true identity. Ask: **Do you sense a need to find your "true identity"? Do you feel you have an identity other than who you say you are or who others say you are?**

4. Direct members to turn to Session 1 Worksheet. Instruct them to answer the question, What do you expect to gain from this study? Have them use the worksheet to record comments of others. Tell students that you will look again at their answers at the last session of the study.

Review This Week's Assignments (5 min.)

1. Say: **Begin to consider an Identity Partner for the study. This person will be a prayer and accountability partner. You will be asked to contact your partner at least weekly during the seven weeks that we are together as a group. We will decide on partners at next week's meeting.**

2. Invite students to memorize the memory verses for week 1, *John 14:20-21.*

3. Ask members to complete week 1 of the study. Hint that you will ask members to share with the group responses identified by the statement, Be prepared to share your response with your Identity Group.

4. Say: **The Identity Group time will be based on your answers and reflections to the response parts of the workbook and the Personal Reflection section. Completing each day's lesson will contribute to the best possible group experience.**

Closing Prayer Time (5 min.)

Invite group members to stand in a circle and hold hands or place arms on each other's shoulders. Ask members to offer a sentence prayer asking God to show them their true identity in Christ.

After the Session: Contact each student before the next meeting. Thank them for joining the group and offer your prayers and support throughout the study. Remind each person of the next meeting.

SESSION 2

Goal: To help students know various ways to identify themselves by being "in Christ."

Opening Prayer (5 min.)

Ask members to share briefly at least one thing they learned during this week's study. Tell students that you will discuss the week in detail later. Share that you want to know what each is learning so group members can rejoice and thank God with them. When all have shared thank God for the lessons learned this week.

Group Interaction Activity (5 min.)

Have each member share answers to the question, "Who am I?" (day 1, p. 9), using the descriptions of Fingerprints, Parentprints, Lifeprints, and Godprints. Then have them share their responses to the activity that asks them to evaluate themselves (day 1, p. 9). Use Session 2 Worksheet to record information shared by members.

Group Sharing (40 min.)

1. Have each member share who they chose as their Identity Partner. If they have not done so allow another week for them to choose. Remind students that this person will pray for them and be an encourager.

2. Ask students to recite the memory verses for week 1, *John 14:20-21.*

3. Ask members to share their answers to Personal Reflection question three, "When I read about the condition of my heart from the words of Jesus, I feel. ..." (day 1, p. 11)

4. Have members share their response to the question, "How do you believe people today would answer the question, 'Who is Jesus?' " (day 2, p. 13). You may want to record answers and then place them on a focal wall.

5. Ask members to form pairs (Identity Partners will work well) and share responses to Personal Reflection question three, "If I were to grade myself (A=excellent; B=average; C=poor) on where I am in the process of being like Jesus, I would give myself a(n) _____ on denying self, a(n) _____ on putting my perceptions and preferences of Jesus on a cross, and a(n) _____ on following Him every day" (day 2, p. 16).

6. Invite each person to share his or her seven descriptive titles (day 3, p. 17).

7. Ask: **Based on your study of the seven ways Jesus described Himself, which one was the freshest to you? Why? What new understanding did you gain from it?**

8. Have each participant share the story behind his or her name or nickname (day 4, p. 21). Invite volunteers to share a name that is special to them and its meaning (day 5, p. 25).

9. Discuss Personal Reflection activity two (day 4, p. 24). Have each member share the name of Jesus they recorded in their Identity Journal and explain why it "struck them."

10. Have participants to share the prayers they wrote to God (day 5, p. 27) asking forgiveness for allowing others' and their own thinking to confuse them about their identity in Him.

Review This Week's Assignments (5 min.)

1. Instruct each member to memorize next week's memory verse. The group will recite the memory verse as part of each week's meeting.

2. Ask participants to complete week 2. Tell students that week 2 is about responding to God's call to follow Him. This involves every aspect of their lives.

3. Encourage students to complete each daily lesson including the Personal Reflection sections.

4. Ask members to pray for each other as they seek to understand their identity in Christ.

Closing Prayer Time (5 min.)

Return to the prayers students wrote to God (day 5, p. 27). Ask them to form pairs and ask God to hear his or her prayer for forgiveness. Ask students to pray that God will help them see themselves as who they are "in Christ." Be prepared to allow anyone who has not trusted Christ to do so during this time.

SESSION 3

Goal: To help students discover and respond to God's call on their lives.

Opening Prayer (5 min.)

Invite members to share a personal need they have identified as a result of the study so far. Pause after each person shares and pray for that need. Close the prayer time asking God to help each member know and respond to God's call on his or her life.

Group Interaction Activity (5 min.)

Have participants turn to page 43 and read the opening illustration for day 4: "Four people stand in front of you—a nurse, a public school teacher, a lawyer, and a pastor. Based on your experiences, which one would you most likely choose as the one who had answered God's call in his or her life?" Ask students to record why they chose the person they did by writing their answers on Session 3 Worksheet. Assure them there is no wrong answer, that you want them to share their understanding of "call" with the group. Ask if their response has changed now that they have completed this week's study.

Group Sharing (40 min.)

1. Ask students to recite the memory verse for week 2, *Ephesians 4:1.*

2. Have members share the name of a person who taught them something significant in their lives (day 1, p. 30). Encourage students to write a note or call that person this week to thank them if they have not done so before.

3. Ask members to share their response to the statement in the margin on page 33, "Your response to God's call is the most transforming event in your life—all else flows from it."

4. Invite members to share responses to the following instructions (day 2, p. 37): "Now go back through the list and place a check beside the question of resistance with which you most identify. Relate that question to what you trust God has called you to do."

5. Ask students to share their responses to Personal Reflection activity four (day 2, p. 38), "If you have already said yes to God's call on your life, what changes have you made in order to do what God has called you to do?" and Personal Reflection activity five (day 2, p. 38), "If you were to say yes to God's call, what changes do you foresee?"

6. Share students' responses to the instruction: "You may have had a similar experience [as the author's] when you thought that if you said yes to God, nothing would ever be the same. Record that experience in the space below" (day 3, p. 40). Be prepared to either pause and pray for each person as responses are shared, or, tell group members you will pray for those who request it at the end of the session.

7. Ask members to share their responses to Personal Reflection activity four (day 3, p. 42), "Has God called you to the same mission as Saul through Jesus' commandment to make disciples of all ethnic groups?"

8. Have students get with their Identity Partners and discuss the areas of their lives that are listed in the margin on page 45 that have separated them from God's call. Lists may include school activities, jobs, home life, or special interests. Ask partners to pray for each other after they have shared together.

9. Ask members to share their responses to: "Go back through this week's lessons and review the biblical characters who said yes to God. Write the name of the one you relate to best and why" (day 5, p. 48).

10. Invite students to share answers to Personal Reflection activity four (day 5, p. 51): "Jesus warned that there is a great cost to following Him. Why is that so? Why do so many people not count the cost before following Jesus?"

Review This Week's Assignments (5 min.)

1. Ask participants to turn to the introduction of week 3 (p. 52) and read the memory verse for the week. Ask them to memorize this verse before the next meeting.

2. Instruct participants to complete week 3. Ask members if anyone is having trouble completing the lessons. If so, ask others to share how they are finding time to complete the study each day. Remind students that their personal study and prayer during the week are what make the Identity Group meeting effective.

3. This week will introduce several new metaphors to describe students' relationships to Christ. Invite them to be open to these biblical ideas in order to understand more fully their lives "in Christ" and the changes that result from that relationship.

4. Invite members to meet with or call their Identity Partner prior to the next meeting. Remind them to pray for and encourage each other.

5. Invite students to keep their Identity Journal up-to-date with what God is teaching them about their identity in Christ.

Closing Prayer Time (5 min.)

Divide into groups of three (not by Identity Partners). Pray for needs identified in the group.

SESSION 4

Goal: To help students acknowledge that change can occur because they are new creations in Christ.

Opening Prayer (5 min.)

This week's study has been about the implications of being a new creation in Christ. Allow each student to voice a prayer of confession of sin's power in his or her life. After everyone has prayed, ask them to thank God for changing and empowering them with a new nature to overcome sin and to live for God. Be prepared to minister to any member who may have a special need or confession.

Group Interaction Activity (5 min.)

Ask members to share their answers to the example about going to the movies on Saturday night (day 5, p. 75). Discuss other habits or interests they discovered they must rethink because of their new life in Christ. Minister to those who may be dealing with sensitive issues.

Group Sharing (40 min.)

1. Ask students to recite the memory verse for week 3, *2 Corinthians 5:17.*

2. Invite members to share what they have experienced or heard others say about faith and the Bible (day 1, p. 54).

3. Say: **Maybe you have experienced some of the frustration Shawn feels toward church and people in the Bible. Or maybe you know someone who has. Do you know a Shawn?** In Romans, Paul described the power of sin in your life without the presence of God. How would you describe what Paul wrote to a person like Shawn?

4. Read *Galatians 5:16-24.* Ask students to share answers to the following questions: "Does your sinful nature allow you to do what you want to do? How does *verse 17* reinforce *Romans 7:14-20?*" (day 2, p. 60); "What are the characteristics of a life that God has filled with His Spirit?" (day 2, p. 61).

5. Ask students to share their responses to Personal Reflection activity three (day 2, p. 62): "When you read about the conflict between your sinful nature and the Spirit, did it remind you of a conflict you have experienced in your life? Briefly describe one experience."

6. Read *Colossians 3:1-2.* Share answers to the questions: "What are some *earthly things* you pursue?"; "What are some *things above* you pursue?" (day 3, p. 64).

7. Complete Session 4 Worksheet.

8. Ask Identity Group members to share with each other about their baptism experience. Be sensitive to those who cannot share about a time when they followed Jesus' in baptism.

9. Invite students to share their personal "doctrine of creation" (day 4, p. 69). Read *2 Corinthians 5:17.* Ask them to share their responses to the instructions: "Describe some of the 'old' that has left your life since you have come into or have grown in your relationship with Jesus." "Describe some of the 'new' ways of living that are part of your life since Jesus came into your heart" (day 4, p. 71).

10. Ask students to share their responses to Personal Reflection activity two (day 5, p. 76): "Reflect on ways your new life in Christ has caused conflict with the lifestyle you experienced prior to putting your faith in Jesus. Ask God to show you ways to resolve those conflicts by allowing your new life desires to overcome old habits."

This Week's Assignments (5 min.)

1. Ask participants to turn to the introduction of week 4 (p. 77) and read the memory verse for the week. Ask them to memorize this verse before the next meeting.

2. Ask participants to complete week 4. Say: **This week you will be studying the biblical concepts of justification, redemption, deliverance, and sanctification as ways to explain your new status before God. You will also discover how you are made holy before God through your relationship with Jesus and how you can overcome temptation in your life.**

3. Encourage students to complete each of the lessons so they can participate fully in next week's session.

Closing Prayer Time (5 min.)

Ask participants to share anything they would like the group to pray with them about that relates to their being a new creation. Invite them to state specific areas that are "old wine skins" that need replacing so the new life in Christ can change them. Pray that each person would allow their new identity and new nature in Christ to grow and to change them.

SESSION 5

Goal: To help students state their new status before God through their relationship with Jesus Christ.

Opening Prayer (5 min.)

Say: **This week we read that you can overcome temptation because you have been delivered from the influence of evil.** Ask members what that means to them. Invite them to pray for God's powerful presence among the group as they discover their new status before God.

Group Interaction Activity (5 min.)

Say: **This week you were introduced to the idea of status and the truth that each of us lives our life before an audience.** Ask students to share the names of people in their lives who are an audience for their actions (day 1, p. 79). Invite them to share what kind of influence these people have on their lives.

Group Sharing (40 min.)

1. Ask students to recite the memory verse for week 4, *Romans 5:10.* Ask them to share what that verse came to mean to them after this week's study.

2. Invite members to record on Session 5 Worksheet the most helpful definitions for the following four key biblical concepts in this session: justification, redemption, deliverance, sanctification.

3. Ask participants to share their answers to the question, "What would change if God were my only audience?" (day 1, p. 79).

4. Review the following Scriptures: *Romans 1:18, Romans 5:10, Galatians 3:10, Ephesians 2:1-5.* Then invite students to respond to the, "What can you conclude about your status before the One who ultimately determines your eternal place?" (day 1, p. 81).

5. Discuss responses to the question, "If the judge were to sentence you in a manner similar to that of the biblical concept of justification, what would it be?" (day 2, p. 83).

6. Invite members to share their definitions of justification (day 2, p. 84).

7. Ask students to share some of their imagined emotions of being held in a hostage situation (day 3, p. 88).

8. Ask members to share their responses to Personal Reflection activity three (day 3, p. 90): "After reading what Jesus' death has done for you, how do you feel about who you are as a person God sees as forgiven, rescued, righteous, and holy? Write a couple of sentences describing how you feel about your identity at this stage of the study."

9. Discuss Personal Reflection activity four (day 3, p. 90): "Describe your feelings about Jesus' death on the cross. Write a letter or poem or paint a picture to express your emotions for God's love and your appreciation to Him for sending His Son to die for you."

10. Say: Day 4 was about overcoming temptation. You may have experienced external temptation. Satan may not have shown up and tempted you in a wilderness, but a person or

opportunity may have tempted you to turn your back on God's goal for your life. Things or people you may have seen or desired can be sources of temptation. Have students share from their lists of ways temptation has come from an external source (day 4, p. 92).

11. Read *Hebrews 4:14-16.* Then ask, **Why can you trust Jesus to understand your situation in the middle of temptation?** (day 4, p. 93).

12. Invite members to share their initial descriptions of sanctification (day 5, p. 96).

13. Read *Hebrews 10:10.* Then discuss how students feel about what Christ has done for them through His death on the cross.

14. Discuss how students' later descriptions of sanctification compare with their initial descriptions (day 5, p. 96 and p. 99).

Review This Week's Assignments (5 min.)

1. Ask participants to turn to the introduction of week 5 (p. 100) and read the memory verse for the week. Ask them to memorize this verse before the next meeting.

2. Say: **During the next week we will study the biblical concepts of adoption, citizenship in heaven, servanthood, and being heirs of God's riches in heaven. Each concept will help us better understand our new standing before God. We will also discover the presence and power of God's Holy Spirit in our lives.** Encourage students to maintain an open heart and mind toward this study.

Closing Prayer Time (5 min.)

Say: **This week's study was about your new status before the One and Holy God. One change in status is that you are made holy by your relationship with Christ.** Close with prayers of thanksgiving for being made holy before God. The group may want to recite *Hebrews 10:10* as their prayer. Ask God to remove things in your lives that prevent you from living holy lives before Him.

SESSION 6

Goal: To help students acknowledge their new standing before God as a result of who they are in Christ.

Opening Prayer (5 min.)

Read *Ephesians 1:13-14* (day 3, p. 110). Ask group members what the verse means to them. During your prayer time, ask God's Spirit to be realized in each participant as a promise of God's salvation in his or her life. Invite students to rejoice because they are "God's possession."

Group Interaction Activity (5 min.)

Say: **This week we learned that we become adopted children of God when we trust Jesus as Lord and Savior.** Ask volunteers to share their answers to the following: "Do you know someone who adopted a child? Maybe you are adopted. What is their, or your, story?" (day 1, p. 102). After all have shared, remind students that the goal of their time together today is to acknowledge their standing before God because of their identity in Christ.

Group Sharing (40 min.)

1. Ask students to recite the memory verse for week 5, *Romans 8:15.*

2. Ask group members to share the letter of thanks they wrote to God for adopting them into His family (day 1, p. 104).

3. Say, **We learned this week about being heirs to God's riches if we are children of God.** Have participants share their ideas about how they would live and what they would do if they were legitimate heirs of Bill Gates, a billionaire (day 2, p. 106).

4. Ask students to describe their inheritances as heirs of God. Discuss feelings about how this truth affects their understanding of their identity in Christ (day 2, p. 107).

5. Say, **We also learned that God's Holy Spirit is a down payment to ensure the believer's inheritance.** Ask members to share answers to the following question, "When was the last time you purchased an item that required a down payment or earnest money?" (day 3, p. 111).

6. Discuss responses to Personal Reflection activity three (day 3, p. 113): "I have been guaranteed I am an heir of God's riches because ..."

7. Say, **Day 4 was about the Christian's standing before God as a citizen of heaven.** Invite members to answer the following questions: "Have you ever traveled to another country? How did you feel? What precautions did you take to protect your passport?" (day 4, p. 114).

8. Ask students to share their answers to the following questions: "Where should your ultimate allegiance be? What rights and privileges can you count on? Which will ultimately be more significant?" (day 4, p. 116).

9. Allow volunteers to complete the statement: "My perception of my standing with God has changed because I learned that in Christ I am ..." (day 5, p. 117).

10. Ask Identity Partners to share with each other their responses to the following: "What things or people do you tend to make masters over your life? Could you call yourself a 'slave' to anything? Are you a slave to sin or to righteousness?" (day 5, p. 119).

11. Pray, taking time to remember those group members identified this week who need this inheritance (day 2, p. 109).

Review This Week's Assignments (5 min.)

1. Ask participants to turn to the introduction of week 6 (p. 121) and read the memory verse for the week. Ask them to memorize this verse before the next meeting.

2. Tell the group that during the next week they will learn how they can be transformed into the likeness of Christ in their everyday lives. They will also discover the implications of being an apprentice to Jesus and how to produce the fruit of God's presence in their lives.

Closing Prayer Time (5 min.)

To conclude your time together, ask members to complete the statements on Session 6 Worksheet that most closely reflects their feelings about what they learned in this week's study. Invite each member to voice a prayer to God using one of the statements they completed from the worksheet.

SESSION 7

Goal: To help students realize the implications that their identity in Christ has on their everyday lives.

Opening Prayer (5 min.)

This is your last session together as a group. Ask members to share the most significant insights they have discovered over the last seven weeks. When all have shared, ask group members to make their statements into prayers of thanksgiving to God for revealing these truths to them. Pray, asking God to allow this time to be the beginning of a life lived as who we really are in Christ.

Group Interaction Activity (5 min.)

Ask participants to respond to: "You may have had someone in your life you imitated. Who is that person, and what have you imitated? If you compared your lives, what would be the same? What would be different?" (day 2, p. 127).

Group Sharing (40 min.)

1. Ask students to recite the memory verses for week 6, *Matthew 7:16-18*.

2. Read *John 15:1-8*. Invite members to share their answers to the following questions: "What analogy does Jesus use in these verses to describe your relationship with Him? What is God's desire for your relationship with Jesus? What is 'fruit' in this passage of Scripture? What is the evidence you are a disciple of Jesus?" (day 1, p. 124).

3. Discuss responses to Personal Reflection activity three: "Explain the difference between change by your efforts and change by God's work in your life. How does that fit with your understanding of what the Bible states about how change happens in a Christian's life? What questions do you have as you seek to change into the likeness of Jesus?" (day 1, p. 125).

4. Ask students to share their lists of ways they can imitate Jesus in their daily lives. Have them share their feelings about being an "apprentice to Jesus" and the implications that kind of relationship has for them (day 2, p. 128). Invite students to record group member's answers on Session 7 Worksheet (p. 159).

5. Ask members to share the list of habits they discovered when they observed Jesus' life from the Gospel of Luke (day 3, p. 133). Encourage students to openly and honestly discuss their lives in comparison and contrast to Jesus' life.

6. Invite members to share their answers to Personal Reflection activity three: "Since you are an apprentice to Jesus, which of the habits you studied today will you begin to develop first? What plan have you written down to help you develop that habit?" (day 3, p. 135).

7. Say, **Two of the lessons we have experienced this week have dealt with "habits that transform."** Discuss the concept of "habits that transform." Then ask members to share the name of someone they admire because that person has excelled in an area they are interested in. What do they know about this person's practice habits? How does this person's practice affect performance? Which habits can they apply to their own lives? (day 4, p. 137).

8. Develop a list of "spiritual workouts" based on how members responded to the question, "What other habits can you identify that God can use to transform you into His likeness" (day 4, p. 139)? It may be a good idea to write the list on a board or large sheet of paper so that all students can see the list.

9. Have members respond to the statement, "the goal of the Christian life is to live up to what you have already attained in your relationship with Christ" (day 5, p. 143). Ask students to share their completed statements, "My identity in Christ is _____, therefore, I commit to live my life to _____." (day 5, p. 144) Discuss ways to "live up to what we have already attained" in Christ (Personal Reflection activity four, p. 145).

10. Ask each participant to return to their statement of expectation written on Session 1 Worksheet (p. 156). Take time to share each expectation and to discuss whether or not it was met during the study.

Closing Prayer Time (10 min.)

Have members gather around one student at a time and say a prayer of encouragement and thanksgiving for that person. Allow time for each individual to experience this. Thank God for revealing each person's identity in Christ and ask Him to work through each member.

Optional Activity: Plan a reunion in six months to see how group members are progressing in living their identity in Christ. The reunion can take the form of a meal, outdoor activity, or meeting, but should allow for discussion, reflection, and prayer.

MY IDENTITY GROUP MEMBERS

Record information shared by your Identity Group members about themselves. Record additional information on the back of this sheet.

Name: _____
Who s/he is: _____
_____

Name: _____
Who s/he is: _____
_____

Name: _____
Who s/he is: _____
_____

Name: _____
Who s/he is: _____
_____

Name: _____
Who s/he is: _____
_____

Name: _____
Who s/he is: _____
_____

Name: _____
Who s/he is: _____
_____

MY IDENTITY IN CHRIST

"On that day you will realize that I am in my Father, and you are in me, and I am in you. Whoever has my commands and obeys them, he is the one who loves me. He who loves me will be loved by my Father, and I too will love him and show myself to him" **(John 14:20-21).**

Answer the question: "What do you expect to gain from this study?"

_____
_____
_____
_____

Record the answers of the other members of your Identity Group.

_____
_____
_____
_____

You will revisit these expectations during session 7.

WHO IS CALLED?

Based on your experiences, which one of the following would you most likely choose as the one who had answered God's call in his or her life? Write your reasons for choosing that person by their title.

○ Nurse

_____
_____
_____
_____
_____

○ Public School Teacher

_____
_____
_____
_____
_____

○ Lawyer

_____
_____
_____
_____
_____

○ Pastor

_____
_____
_____
_____
_____

ON THINGS ABOVE

Create the following two lists with the help of members of your Identity Group.

What I can do to set my **heart** on things above:

_____
_____
_____
_____
_____
_____
_____

What I can do to set my **mind** on things above:

_____
_____
_____
_____
_____
_____
_____

MY STATUS BEFORE GOD

Record the most helpful definitions for the key biblical concepts of justification, redemption, deliverance, and sanctification. Record the thoughts of other members of your Identity Group.

Justification

_____
_____
_____
_____
_____

Redemption

_____
_____
_____
_____
_____

Deliverance

_____
_____
_____
_____
_____

Sanctification

_____
_____
_____

GOD, I THANK YOU ...

Complete one of the following statements as a prayer to God.

"God, I thank You for adopting me as Your child. Since I am Your child, I ..."

_____
_____
_____

"God, I thank You for making me a coheir with Christ of Your riches. Since I am Your heir, I ..."

_____
_____
_____

"God, I thank You for making me a citizen of heaven. Since I am a citizen of heaven, I ..."

_____
_____
_____

"God, I thank You for ensuring my inheritance of salvation by giving me Your Holy Spirit. Since Your Spirit lives in me, I ..."

_____
_____
_____

"God, I thank You for allowing me to be your servant. Since I am a servant of God, I ..."

_____
_____

AN APPRENTICE TO JESUS

Record responses from your Identity Group members as they share their list of ways they can imitate Jesus in their daily lives. This will include behaviors, thoughts, and habits learned from Jesus.

1. _____

2. _____

3. _____

4. _____

5. _____

6. _____

7. _____

8. _____

9. _____

10. _____

11. _____

12. _____

13. _____

14. _____

15. _____

Two Ways to Earn Credit
for Studying LifeWay Christian Resources Material

CHRISTIAN GROWTH STUDY PLAN

Christian Growth Study Plan resources are available for course credit for personal growth and church leadership training.

Courses are designed as plans for personal spiritual growth and for training current and future church leaders. To receive credit, complete the book, material, or activity. Respond to the learning activities or attend group sessions, when applicable, and show your work to your pastor, staff member, or church leader. Then go to *www.lifeway.com/CGSP,* or call the toll-free number for instructions for receiving credit and your certificate of completion.

For information about studies in the Christian Growth Study Plan, refer to the current catalog online at the CGSP Web address. This program and certificate are free LifeWay services to you.

CONTACT INFORMATION:
Christian Growth Study Plan
One LifeWay Plaza, MSN 117
Nashville, TN 37234
CGSP info line 1-800-968-5519
www.lifeway.com/CGSP
To order resources 1-800-458-2772

Need a CEU?

Receive Continuing Education Units (CEUs) when you complete group Bible studies by your favorite LifeWay authors.

CONTACT INFORMATION:
CEU Coordinator
One LifeWay Plaza, MSN 150
Nashville, TN 37234
Info line 1-800-968-5519
www.lifeway.com/CEU

Some studies are approved by the Association of Christian Schools International (ACSI) for CEU credits. Do you need to renew your Christian school teaching certificate? Gather a group of teachers or neighbors and complete one of the approved studies. Then go to *www.lifeway.com/CEU* to submit a request form or to find a list of ACSI-approved LifeWay studies and conferences. Book studies must be completed in a group setting. Online courses approved for ACSI credit are also noted on the course list. The administrative cost of each CEU certificate is only $10 per course.